EVERYTHING IN THE SHOP WANTS TO KILL YOU

(AND HOW TO STOP IT)

A KNIFEMAKER'S GUIDE TO SHOP SAFETY

NATE "TUNA" GRANT

Contents

Introduction

Welcome to the Knife Shop (and Surviving It)

Every knifemaker, blacksmith, or metalworker eventually realizes the same truth. The shop is not a safe place. The forge breathes fire. The grinder eats steel and will happily chew on you too. The dust in the air may smell good or exotic, but it is often worse for your lungs than anything you will ever smoke.

This book exists because we makers want to keep making. We do not want injuries or hospital trips cutting that short. And if we are honest, most of us do not learn the lessons until we have already been nicked, burned, or nearly shocked. My hope is that this book catches you before the "nearly" turns into "actually."

I did not set out to be a safety expert. I set out to be a maker. A guy in a shop who loves steel, fire, wood, and the endless challenge of turning raw material into something useful and beautiful. What qualifies me to write this book is not a stack of safety certifications. It is scars, close calls, and a stubborn streak of curiosity. Yes, I do hold certifications, and while they are valuable they do not exempt me from learning or from making mistakes. Certifications do not stop a grinder belt from breaking or a forge from running hot. They just give me one more tool to understand what is happening when they do.

That said, I do recommend pursuing certifications or safety classes yourself. They do not just help you. They make your shop safer, improve your confidence, and ultimately strengthen your end product. Knowledge multiplies. The more you learn, the less you lose; time, money, or fingers. This book is just as much for me as it is for you. I need the reminders. I need the lists. I need the checkmarks on the wall. Think of it less like a lecture and more like sitting down with a fellow maker who admits, "Yeah, I have made the dumb mistakes too." Let us figure out how to do better together. This is meant to be a guide to help our craft grow from generation to generation. Just because many of us old guys grew up in the school of hard knocks and extreme common sense does not mean we cannot learn new things or be reminded of what matters. The shop is not static. It evolves. Materials change, tools change, and so should our safety practices.

Knifemakers are a stubborn bunch. We pride ourselves on figuring things out. We do not like being told what to do. And most of us secretly believe we are tougher than we really are. But stubbornness does not protect you from sparks landing in an oily rag, from a belt breaking at full speed, or from the silent creep of wood dust in your lungs. This book does not exist to take away your independence. It exists to protect it.

This book is divided into nine sections. Each one is built around the real-life hazards of a working shop.

1. General Shop Safety. The foundation: layout, organization, lighting, PPE, and fire readiness.

2. Tool Safety. The machines that bite back: grinders, saws, presses, forges, welders, and more.

3.   Material Handling and Disposal. The hidden hazards in steel, wood, synthetics, dust, and chemicals.

4.   Woodworking and Handles. Where the knife meets the hand. Dust, adhesives, finishes, and fine work.

5.   First Aid and Medical Response. Cuts, burns, eyes, chemicals, and what to do when it goes wrong.

6.   Electrical Safety. The invisible danger: cords, breakers, wiring, and what to do when it fails.

7.   Personal Considerations. Mental health, physical fitness, clothing, working alone, mindset.

8.   Special Considerations. Apprentices, kids, visitors, pets, insurance, liabilities.

9.   Reference Materials. Checklists, charts, emergency plans, SDS guides. Quick access when you do not have time to think.

Together, these are not just rules. They are habits. The habits that make your shop productive instead of destructive.

At the end of the day, this is not about making you too scared to work in the shop. It is about making you consistent. The safer you are, the longer you get to create. A cluttered shop slows you down. A bad injury stops you cold. A fire can take away everything you have built. Safety is not what kills momentum. It is what lets you keep it for years, even decades. And if this book helps even one new or seasoned maker avoid injury and keep growing the craft, it has done its job.

You will laugh at some of this. You will nod at other parts. And sometimes you will roll your eyes and think, "That will never happen to me." That is fine. Just remember, every scar in this book was once owned by someone who thought the same thing. So let us step into the shop together with glasses on, respirator ready, and extinguisher nearby. With the right mindset we will walk back out at the end of the day with all ten fingers, both eyes, and the satisfaction of a craft well practiced.

One last note before we begin. You will notice repetitions sprinkled throughout this book. They are there on purpose. They reinforce the concept of safety and continually hammer the same thought home so you remember it. These pages are here to drive conversations and make you think. You can also use this book as a guide when in discussions at classes or get-togethers. Share the pages, talk through the checklists, and keep the craft growing stronger together.

Welcome to the shop. Let this keep you in one piece.

General Shop Safety

Step into any knife shop and you will notice two things right away: the tools are powerful, and there are hazards everywhere. Sparks, sharp edges, flammable rags, grinding dust, heavy stock, chemical fumes, etc.; all of them waiting for a human mistake. There is a simple reality in this kind of environment. Accidents do not just happen, they wait to happen. It is up to you to recognize the dangers and prepare yourself to avoid them. The purpose of this section is not to alarm you but to prepare you. General safety is not about slowing you down, and it is not a box to check before the "real" work starts. It is about making sure you can walk out of the shop at the end of the day with all your fingers, your eyesight, your hearing, and your lungs intact. Think of it this way: every injury that is avoided, every fire prevented, every clean breath of air, is what keeps this craft sustainable for years to come.

Rule #1: Everything in your shop is trying to kill you.

That may sound dramatic, but it is the right mindset to carry into the shop. The grinder does not care how careful you think you are, it is hungry and wants to eat whatever you feed it. The buffer? More knifemakers have been injured or killed by buffers than by forges or hammers. Dust does not look dangerous, but it will suffocate you slowly. Solvents and oily rags do not need your help to catch fire. Your eyeballs? They are about as tough as skinned grapes. We could go on and on with these sayings, but when you accept the concept that everything has the potential to hurt you, safety stops being an afterthought. It becomes a natural thought process. It becomes common sense.

There are many, many stories of accidents that have happened in the shop. You may have personally experienced some accidents yourself. How do you respond when you are hearing or talking about accidents from the shop? What is the point of sharing or hearing these experiences? We tell them because we want to remind each other about the need for a safety mindset in our shops. There are many horror stories from makers over the years. A knifemaker was killed in his own shop when a buffer caught a blade and ripped it out of his hands, the blade lodged in his chest before he could react. A small custom maker's shop burned to the ground because sparks from an angle grinder settled into a dust collector. The fire did not start immediately; it smoldered for hours before erupting long after the maker had gone home. By the time the fire department arrived, the shop was gone. A hobbyist left a pile of linseed oil-soaked rags in a plastic bucket overnight. By morning, spontaneous combustion had started, and the garage was a total loss. Another maker reached for a piece of steel near the grinder while wearing gloves. The belt grabbed the glove instantly, pulling his hand into the machine. He survived, but with permanent damage and limited hand function. These stories are not "rare" accidents; they are common enough that at every knife show or get together, someone has a story to tell. Learn from them before they happen to you. Take the time to listen, to understand what went wrong and how it could have been prevented. Shop accidents are not badges of honor. The goal is to prevent accidents so we can continue to do the things that we love to do.

Walking into a bare blade in the vise is a mistake you only make once. Cover it.

A safe shop is not built on a single rule or tool. It is a series of overlapping layers that all work together. Setting up the way your tools, benches, and pathways are arranged is either working for you or against you. Working safely cannot happen if you do not see clearly or breathe cleanly. Shadows hide sharp edges. Dust contaminates your lungs. Cluttered shops are much slower to move around in; they are also fire and trip hazards. A clean bench and a swept floor prevent more accidents than you would ever expect. A fire can eliminate your entire shop in minutes. Preparation, extinguishers, and daily habits are what stand between you and disaster. Together, these layers and many others create resilience. If one fails, another catches you. They only work if you take the time, put in the effort, and create a safe shop. The real difference between a safe shop and an accident waiting to happen is not how many rules are posted on the wall; it is the mindset of the person working. Safe shops are built on habits: automatically putting on glasses when you walk in. Putting tools back in their place instead of leaving them on the bench. Sweeping the floor at the end of every day. Checking dust bins and unplugging machines before you turn out the lights. These are small actions, but if practiced daily, they build a shop culture where safety is natural. It is tempting to cut corners. "Just one cut without glasses." "I'll clean the bench later." "That rag pile isn't big enough to worry about." But neglect adds up, and eventually it costs you. A trip to the ER is expensive. Permanent hearing loss is irreversible. Nothing slows down your work or drains your wallet like an injury that could have been prevented with a simple habit. Protecting yourself is the last line of defense when something does go wrong. It does not prevent mistakes, but it makes the difference between a close call and a life-altering injury. To have a safe shop with limited injuries, you must make the choice that you will do what it takes to think through the layers of safety.

There is a reason this manual mixes in humor. Knife makers are independent, stubborn, and sometimes allergic to "safety talk." Humor helps to make these lessons stick. You will remember the comicality about your eyeballs being like skinned grapes, and that might be the reason you grab your safety glasses next time. The point is not to make light of safety; it is to make it memorable. If you remember the humor, you remember the rule.

This section lays the groundwork for every other part of the manual. It is divided into five pillars of general shop safety:

Shop Layout & Organization (1.1): Setting up your space for safety and efficiency.

Lighting & Ventilation (1.2): Seeing clearly and breathing clean air.

Housekeeping & Cleanliness (1.3): Keeping hazards from building up unnoticed.

Personal Protective Equipment (1.4): Your last line of defense.

Fire Safety (1.5): Preparing for, and preventing, the most destructive shop hazard.

These topics may not be glamorous, but they are the foundation. Master them, and everything else from forging to grinding to finishing becomes safer, smoother, and more sustainable.

> That extension cord across the floor? It's waiting to trip you while you're carrying hot steel.

Section 1.1 – Shop Layout & Organization

A well organized shop is your first line of defense against accidents. Most injuries do not happen because of dramatic machinery failures, they happen because somebody tripped, slipped, or bumped into something sharp. Safety is not the only benefit. A well organized shop becomes more efficient, and efficiency produces a better end product. When tools are where they should be and your workflow is smooth, you spend less time fumbling, less energy moving around, and more time focused on the craft.

Whether you have a large shop, a garage, or a corner of the basement, layout matters. Good organization keeps you out of the ER and keeps your knives out of the scrap pile.

Shop Layout Basics

- Clear, wide walking paths free of cords, scrap, and clutter.
- Work zones grouped logically (forge → anvil → quench → grinder → finishing).
- Adequate floor space around each machine (no "squeeze-by" setups).
- Heavy tools (anvils, grinders, presses) anchored or on stable bases.
- Blades clamped in vises covered with backing boards/guards when not being worked.
- Electrical cords managed. No extension cords across walkways.
- Emergency shutoffs (breaker box, power strips) easy to reach.
- Common-use tools stored at arm's reach, specialty tools stowed out of the way.

Workflow Efficiency

- Forge-to-Grind Line: Arrange the forge, anvil, quench, and grinder so hot steel moves in a straight path without carrying it across the entire shop.
- Handle/Finish Zone: Woodworking, adhesives, and sanding belong together in a "clean zone," far from sparks and scale.
- Finishing Zone: Oils, waxes, and buffers grouped together prevent you from running across the shop with oily rags.
- First Reach Rule: The tools you use every day should live within arm's reach of their workstation.

Rule: If space forces you to compromise, never compromise on clear walkways or fire safety.

"It's just a scratch" is the official last words of many fine makers.

Floor & Surfaces

- Concrete is best (durable, fire-safe).

- Anti-fatigue mats reduce strain, but do not place them where sparks or hot steel fall.

- Workbench height: around elbow level for comfort and control.

- Keep benches dedicated to current projects not storage piles.

Tool Storage & Safety

- Use blade covers, backing boards, or racks. Do not leave edges exposed.

- Store materials near their point of use (steel by the forge, wood by the woodworking bench).

- Shadow boards or labeled drawers make it obvious when tools are missing.

- Arrange heavy or sharp tools so you are not walking across the shop juggling them.

Power & Electrical Considerations

- Install outlets close to each machine to avoid extension cords.

- Use heavy-duty, grounded cords if extension cords are unavoidable.

- Rule: If your wiring was done by "that guy who's handy," get it inspected by a real electrician.

Benefits Of Efficiency

- Less fatigue: Shorter walks and fewer wasted motions.

- Fewer mistakes: Disorganized shops create distractions, and distractions create accidents.

- Higher output: Organized shops produce more, faster.

- Cleaner knives: Efficiency prevents contamination (sawdust in epoxy, corrosion on steel, neutralization solution in acid).

Small Shop & Limited Space Notes

- Multi-use benches: Dedicate one sturdy bench to multiple tasks but enforce a clean reset between operations.

- Portable tools: Mount grinders, buffers, and small presses on rolling carts or bench plates.

- Vertical storage: Pegboards, wall racks, and shelving reduce bench clutter and free floor space.

- Efficiency by sequence: In a small shop, organize your work by order of operations instead of zones.

> If you spend more time looking for your hammer than swinging it, your layout needs work.

Section 1.2 – Lighting & Ventilation

Good light and clean air are two things most knife makers do not consider until they are not available. Poor lighting means you cannot see what you are doing, which leads to crooked grinds, uneven bevels, or worse. Without proper lighting you may miss the fact that your hand is too close to the belt. Poor ventilation is even more insidious: dust, fumes, and smoke build up slowly. While you may not notice in the moment, your lungs, sinuses, and long-term health absolutely will. Lighting and ventilation are not luxuries, they are safety multipliers. A brightly lit, well-ventilated shop keeps you more alert, reduces mistakes, and protects you from invisible hazards.

Lighting

General Lighting

- Overhead lights should evenly illuminate the shop floor with no dark corners.

- LEDs are best: bright, low heat, long life, and low power draw.

- Position fixtures so machines cast minimal shadows. Lights should come from above and slightly in front of work areas.

Task Lighting

- Adjustable lamps at the grinder, drill press, vise, and finishing bench.

- Magnifying lamps are invaluable for detail work (file work, inlay, polishing).

- Mount a directional light at about a 45° angle to highlight the scratch pattern on bevels.

Emergency Lighting

- Keep a rechargeable shop light or headlamp handy. Carrying hot steel or being mid-cut in darkness is a recipe for disaster.

- If your shop has no windows, install at least one battery-powered emergency light.

Efficiency means finishing knives not finding yourself in the ER.

Ventilation

Dust & Particulates

- Grinding, sanding, and buffing create fine dust. The particles you cannot see are the most dangerous.

- Exotic woods (like cocobolo, rosewood, ebony, etc.) can trigger severe allergic or toxic reactions.

- [Synthetics (G10, micarta, carbon fiber, etc.) produce microscopic shards that damage lungs and skin.

- Use a dust collector or shop vac with a HEPA filter at grinders and sanders.

Fumes & Chemicals

- Epoxies, solvents, and finishes release vapors that irritate eyes, skin, and lungs and may ignite near sparks.

- Etching acids (ferric chloride, muriatic, etc.) must never be used in unventilated spaces.

- Forge and welding fumes contain carbon monoxide (odorless, invisible, and deadly) Install a CO detector.

Airflow

- The goal: move dirty air out and bring fresh air in.

- Cross-ventilation (fan pulling air in, fan exhausting air out) works best.

- A single fan just stirring air is not enough, it only spreads dust evenly.

Respiratory Protection

- Dust mask = bare minimum. Respirator = recommended.

- Half-mask respirators with P100 filters are best for particulates.

- Add organic vapor cartridges for solvents, epoxy, or finishes.

- Fit is critical — facial hair can compromise the seal.

Rule: If you can smell it or taste it, your protection isn't working.

Sparks & Fire Hazards In Ventilation

- Dust + Sparks = Fire. Wood dust, micarta, or G10 dust can ignite.

- A single glowing ember from a grinder can smolder in a dust collector for hours before igniting.

- Shop vacuums can catch fire if sparks enter the hose or filter.

If you can't see the edge, you'll probably feel it the hard way.

Prevention Tips

- Never let sparks feed directly into a dust collector.

- Use spark arrestors, water traps, or baffles between grinders and collection hoses.

- Empty dust bins often — do not store weeks of "spark fuel."

- Keep collectors in nonflammable enclosures if possible.

- Always shut down collection systems when leaving the shop.

Rule: If your dust collector smells "hot," investigate immediately. Fires in dust systems are a known cause of shop losses.

Benefits Of Good Lighting & Ventilation

- Better visibility = cleaner grinds, safer cuts, fewer surprises.

- Clean air = fewer long-term respiratory problems.

- Comfortable environment = less fatigue and better focus.

Small Shop Notes

If you cannot afford a full dust system, prioritize:

- A fan exhausting air out through a window or vent.

- A HEPA air purifier or box fan with furnace filter.

- Portable dust shrouds on grinders and sanders.

- Do sanding of exotic woods or G10 outdoors if possible.

Dust doesn't look scary, but it'll kill you slower and quieter than fire.

Section 1.3 – Housekeeping & Cleanliness

Most accidents in a knife shop do not come from catastrophic tool failures, they come from the everyday hazards that build up when the shop is not kept clean. Dust, oily rags, cords across the floor, and benches cluttered with sharp edges all combine into a dangerous environment. Good housekeeping is not about keeping your shop "Instagram ready". It is about removing the hazards that accumulate slowly and quietly. A clean, orderly shop reduces trip hazards, prevents fires, protects your lungs, and keeps you focused on your work. Think of every piece of clutter as something waiting for the right moment to trip you, cut you, or catch fire.

Floors & Walkways

- Keep walkways open. Cords, clamps, buckets, and scrap steel do not belong underfoot.

- Mop or absorb spills immediately. Slipping while holding hot steel is a nightmare scenario.

- Sweep or vacuum regularly to clear scale, grit, dust, and shavings that cause slips.

- Store long stock (bars, pipe, wood blanks) in racks or along walls, never across walkways.

Benches & Work Surfaces

- Limit benchtops to the project at hand. Yesterday's scraps and tools belong in storage.

- Wipe down after glue-ups, finishing, or sanding. Dust, epoxy, and oils easily transfer to new work.

- Never leave bare blades loose on benches. Use guards, sheaths, bins, or racks.

Dust & Debris Management

- Metal dust + wood dust + sparks = fire fuel. Always clean between grinding and woodworking operations. Wood dust will almost always ignite with sparks.

- Sweeping stirs fine dust into the air. Vacuum with HEPA filtration whenever possible.

- Keep wood dust and metal dust separate if possible. Mixing them increases fire and explosion risk.

- Empty dustbins and shop vacuums regularly. Steel embers can smolder long after grinding stops.

Grinder sparks don't care if your vacuum was $50 or $500, they'll still light it up.

Rags & Combustibles

- Oily rags (linseed, tung, Danish oils, etc.) can spontaneously combust. Store in a sealed metal container.

- Solvent rags should be stored separately and never crumpled in a pile. Spread flat outside to dry if disposal is delayed.

- Keep solvents, oils, and adhesives in metal safety cans or fire-rated cabinets, not on open shelves.

Tool & Material Storage

- Tools should live in racks, drawers, or shadow boards, not scattered around.

- Sheaths, covers, bins, or racks keep knives from cutting you when you are not working on them.

- Steel stock belongs near the forge, wood blocks near the woodworking bench, chemicals in a sealed cabinet.

Electrical & Plugged-In Hazards

- Unplug idle tools. Grinders, buffers, and saws should be disconnected when not in use for an extended time. A bumped switch can turn them into instant hazards.

- Hand tools should be unplugged immediately after completion of the task.

- Lithium-ion and NiMH battery chargers (for lights, tools, etc.) can overheat or fail if left plugged in unattended. Fires have flared up this way. Unplug chargers when charging is finished or not in use.

- Do not leave multiple extension cords coiled under benches plugged in. Heat buildup + dust = ignition risk.

Rule: If you are not in the shop, your tools and chargers should not be drawing power.

End-Of-Day Routine

- Sweep floors and clear benchtops.

- Empty dust bins, trash cans, and rag cans if they contain flammables.

- Check that all tools are unplugged or switched off.

- Close up with a "fire walk" — look for glowing embers, heat, or suspicious smells before shutting down. Do this even if you have not fired up the forge or used the grinder.

- Make it a habit to thoroughly check your shop before closing up!

- At a minimum, always do a visual walk through the shop before closing.

Your grinder is hungry enough, don't feed it your lungs too.

Benefits Of Good Housekeeping

- Safer floors = fewer trips and slips.

- Fewer combustibles = lower fire risk.

- Cleaner benches = fewer cuts and less contamination.

- More efficient workflow = more knives finished, less time wasted.

- Professional pride: your shop reflects your discipline.

Small Shop Notes

- Limited storage = faster clutter. Rotate projects, finish one before starting another.

- Pegboards, hooks, and wall-mounted racks can double your usable space.

- Rolling carts help store portable tools and keep walkways clear.

Every scrap of steel on the floor is a tripwire with your name on it.

Section 1.4 – Personal Protective Equipment (PPE) Basics

If shop layout and housekeeping are the foundation of safety, PPE is your armor. It is the last barrier between you and the hundreds of little ways a knife shop tries to injure you. In a single session you may face sparks, hot steel, flying debris, razor-sharp edges, grinding dust, toxic fumes, chemical splashes, noise, and heat. Each hazard alone is serious. Together, they are relentless. PPE does not make you invincible and it does not replace smart shop habits or good workflow. What it does is buy you time and a margin for error. The best PPE turns serious accidents into minor inconveniences. Safety glasses turn a flying shard into a blink instead of blindness. Earplugs turn a day at the grinder into a night of sleep without ringing. A respirator keeps today's fine dust from becoming tomorrow's permanent lung disease. Many makers skip PPE out of impatience, discomfort, or the "just this once" mindset. But ask anyone who has been injured or who has experienced an irreversible injury. The few seconds it takes to put on gear is nothing compared to weeks of lost shop time, hospital bills, or permanent damage.

Rule #1: PPE is not optional gear — it is part of the uniform.

Eye & Face Protection

- Safety Glasses: Non-negotiable. Always wear impact-rated (ANSI Z87+) glasses. Keep multiple pairs around the shop at all times.

- Face Shields: Required for grinding, buffing, and lathe work. They go over safety glasses, never in place of them.

- Chemical Goggles: Sealed goggles when working with acids, ferric chloride, or solvents.

- Maintenance: Replace scratched or cracked lenses. Clean with mild soap, not harsh solvents that weaken plastic.

- Storage: Keep in a clean spot. Hanging them on a nail next to the grinder guarantees scratches.

Note: The koozies everyone likes to give away make great "eyeglass cases".

Rule: Your eyeballs are about as tough as skinned grapes. Protect them accordingly.

That pile of oily rags isn't "shop character", it's a future bonfire.

Hearing Protection

Hazards: Grinders, power hammers, presses, and saws hit decibel levels that permanently damage hearing in minutes.

Options:

- Foam earplugs: cheap, disposable, effective.
- Over-ear protection: reusable, quick to put on/off.
- Electronic muffs: amplify conversation but clamp down on loud impact noise.
- Fit: Plugs must be rolled, compressed, and fully inserted. Halfway in = no protection.

Maintenance: Replace foam plugs often; clean or replace earmuff cushions if cracked.

Rule: Protect your ears now so you can still hear compliments on your knives later.

Respiratory Protection

Masks vs. Respirators:

- Paper dust masks give minimal protection. Do not trust them for grinding or sanding.
- Half-mask respirators with P100 filters are the standard for metal and wood dust.
- Add organic vapor cartridges for epoxies, acetone, or finishes.

Critical Hazards:

- G10, micarta, carbon fiber creates glassy splinters that damage your lungs.
- Exotic hardwoods can cause allergic reactions and long-term respiratory illnesses.
- Fine metal dust equates to long-term lung damage.

Rule: Seal is critical for respiratory protection. Beards or stubble prevent proper fit. Either trim the mask zone or use a powered air-purifying respirator (PAPR).

Maintenance:

- Replace filters when breathing becomes difficult or odor seeps through.
- Store respirators in sealed bags when not in use.

Rule: If you can smell it or taste it, your filter is not working.

Messy benches don't build knives; they build ER bills.

Hand Protection

When Gloves Help:

- Heat-resistant gloves: handling hot steel, quenching, or working near forges.
- Nitrile gloves: epoxy, acids, solvents, and finishing oils.

When Gloves Kill:

- Never use gloves around grinders, buffers, lathes, or drill presses. These machines grab fast, and gloves can pull your hand straight in.

Note: Cut resistant gloves can be a great addition to your PPE. Be sure to understand the different ratings available.

Forging Note: Hammer control comes from feel. Many smiths avoid gloves on the hammer hand. Use callus, chalk, or hammer wraps instead.

Maintenance:

- Replace heat rated gloves when scorched or worn.
- Dispose of nitrile gloves after use.

Rule: Gloves are tools, not armor. Use them for specific jobs, not all jobs.

Clothing & Aprons

- Safe Fabrics: Cotton, denim, wool, leather, heavy canvas.
- Unsafe Fabrics: Polyester, nylon, or synthetics. They will melt and stick to your skin from heat or sparks.
- Aprons: Leather or canvas aprons protect against sparks, hot steel, and flying debris.
- Fit: No baggy sleeves, dangling strings, or frayed cuffs. They love to snag in machines.
- Maintenance: Wash shop clothes separately; solvents and metal dust do not belong in household laundry.

Forge Note: Athletic "moisture-wicking" shirts are comfortable, but in the forging area, they are a skin-melting hazard.

If you leave your angle grinder plugged in, it's just waiting for the cat, your kid, or your elbow to turn it on.

Foot Protection

- Basics: Closed-toe shoes always. Leather boots are best.
- Steel Toe: Strongly recommended for anvils, presses, and heavy billets of steel.
- Slip Resistance: Floors get slick with oil, water, or quench spills. Good tread is a lifesaver.
- Maintenance: Replace boots with worn soles. Dry thoroughly.
- Wet boots + extension cords = electrocution hazard.

Rule: Hot steel on toes equates to the shop day over.

Head Protection

- Welding Helmets: Auto-darkening helmets protect from flash burns and UV. Always check batteries before starting.
- Hard Hats: Not always needed in small shops, but smart if storing heavy stock overhead.
- Caps: A simple cotton cap under a face shield helps protect scalp and hair from sparks.

PPE Maintenance & Habits

- Keep PPE in one central, clean location. If it is buried under clutter, you will not use it.
- Check Before Use: Inspect glasses, shields, filters, straps, and gloves. Replace anything cracked, fogged, scratched, or worn out.
- PPE has a lifespan. Filters clog, plastics weaken, and gloves wear thin from use. Do not wait for failure to replace.
- Habit Building: Put PPE where you cannot miss it. Hang glasses on the grinder, keep earplugs by the anvil, etc...
- Visitors: No PPE = no entry. Keep spares for apprentices, friends, or curious neighbors.

Benefits Of PPE

- Turns catastrophic hazards into minor inconveniences.
- Shields you from invisible, long-term risks like hearing loss, lung damage, and chemical sensitization.
- Reinforces discipline — PPE use becomes second nature.

No gloves around machines. EVER. Unless you want to find out how much like toothpaste your hand really is.

Small Shop Notes

Prioritize PPE purchases:

- Safety glasses
- Respirator
- Hearing protection
- Gloves/aprons/boots

Note: If cost is a concern, buy multiples of the cheapest but most critical items — glasses and earplugs.

If you're too cool for safety glasses, you'll look even cooler with a pirate patch.

Section 1.5 – Fire Safety

A knife shop is one of the most fire-prone workspaces you can be in. Open flames, glowing steel, sparks, flammable dust, solvent-soaked rags, and electrical loads all share the same space. That means a fire hazard is present every minute you are working and often after you have shut everything down. Many shop fires do not happen while you are standing at the grinder, they start quietly and spread after you leave the shop. A single spark that settles into a dust collector, an oily rag tossed into the corner, or a forgotten tool left running can ignite into flames hours later. By morning, your shop could be gone. Fire safety is not about fear; it is about preparation. The goal is to prevent fire where possible, catch it early if it starts, and limit the damage if it grows. How can you achieve that goal? By controlling hazards, keeping the right equipment in place, and knowing exactly how to react if a fire happens.

Fire Extinguishers

Types to keep on hand:

- Class ABC (general purpose): Effective on wood, paper, most shop combustibles, flammable liquids, and electrical fires.

- Class D: Required if you work with reactive metals such as magnesium, titanium, aluminum, or zirconium. These metals burn at extreme heat and can react violently with water or ABC extinguishers.

- CO2 Extinguishers: Effective for electrical fires and solvents. Not a replacement for ABC or D, but useful for clean suppression.

Placement:

- Minimum of two extinguishers: one near the hot work area (forge/grinders), one near the exit.

- Mount on walls in visible, accessible spots.

- Never store on the floor or behind benches.

Maintenance:

- Check gauges monthly.

- Service or replace expired extinguishers.

- Replace or recharge immediately after any use.

Respirator rule: breathe through the filter, not through your lungs.

Fire Hazards In Knife Shops

- Sparks & embers: grinding, cutting, and welding throw showers of sparks. Even a single glowing ember can ignite wood dust, paper, or oily debris hours later.

- Oily rags & combustible waste: rags soaked in linseed, tung, Danish oil, or other drying oils can self-ignite. Solvent rags can ignite if left crumpled in piles.

- Dust & dust collectors: Fine wood dust, micarta, and G10 particles are combustible. Shop vacuums and collectors can smolder for hours if embers enter filters or bins.

- Specialty metals:
    - Magnesium: sparks and dust ignite easily, burning hotter than steel. Water makes magnesium fires worse.
    - Titanium: chips and dust can ignite under friction. These react violently with oxidizers.
    - Aluminum: dust is highly combustible and explosive in air.

- Flammable liquids & chemicals: acetone, denatured alcohol, epoxy hardeners, finishes, and adhesives are all fire hazards. Improper storage or open containers near sparks invite disaster.

- Electrical hazards: overloaded circuits, undersized extension cords, and battery chargers plugged in can overheat and ignite.

Rule: always segregate reactive metal dust and chips. Never collect them with wood dust.

Prevention Habits

- Sweep and vacuum regularly to reduce fuel buildup.

- Always use spark arrestors or baffles if grinding into dust collectors.

- Empty dust bins daily if reactive or mixed dust is present.

- Store rags in sealed metal containers. Never toss them in open trash cans.

- Keep solvents and adhesives in fire-rated cabinets or safety cans.

- Do not store propane, acetylene, or oxygen cylinders inside enclosed shops.

- Check wiring and outlets. If cords are warm to the touch, they are overloaded.

- End every day with a "fire walk": check rags, bins, outlets, and machines before leaving.

Steel-toe boots: because flip-flops are for the beach, not the forge.

Material Safety Data Sheets (Sds/Msds)

What they are:

- SDS sheets are standardized documents that provide critical information about every chemical or substance, its hazards, safe handling, storage, protective measures, and emergency procedures.

Why they matter:

- SDS sheets tell you exactly how flammable a material is, how to handle it safely, what protective gear to use, and what to do in the case of an emergency

- Every chemical, finish, adhesive, material, and solvent has an SDS sheet with its details.

Access:

- SDS sheets can be found on the manufacturer's website, from the supplier you get your materials from, or by searching the product name plus SDS on the web.

- Keep printed SDS sheets in a binder in the shop.

- Organize by category (finishes, solvents, adhesives, acids).

Critical notes from SDS:

- Flash points (temperature at which vapors ignite).

- Proper extinguishers to use.

- Storage limits (temperature and container type).

- Proper PPE

- 1st aid recommendations

Rule: If you cannot explain how to put out a fire involving a chemical you are using, you have not read the SDS.

Emergency Response

- Know your extinguishers: use the PASS method — Pull, Aim, Squeeze, Sweep. Always aim at the base of flames.

- Size up: if the fire is spreading beyond a small area, or you do not have the right extinguisher, escape immediately.

- Exit strategy: keep exits clear. A path blocked with stock or clutter wastes precious seconds.

- After extinguishing: monitor the area. Charred wood or materials, dust, or rags can reignite.

If your apron smells like bacon after forging, that was you cooking.

Benefits Of Fire Safety

- Prevents catastrophic loss of shop, home, or life.

- It makes daily work safer. The discipline of a consistent "fire walk" reinforces other safety habits.

- A peace of mind when leaving the shop at night.

Small Shop Notes

- In garages or basements, a single fire can endanger your whole home. Do not cut corners.

- Keep at least one extinguisher near the forge and one by the door.

- Consider a fire blanket for smothering clothing or bench-top fires.

- Smoke alarms and CO detectors should be standard in every shop.

A clean shop doesn't just look better, it burns slower.

Tool Safety

In every knife shop, the tools are the heartbeat. From the simplest hammer to the loudest grinder, tools shape raw steel into something useful, beautiful, and lasting. But they also shape the maker. Sometimes the lessons arrive the hard way. Every scar, every trip to the ER, and every story that starts with "I will never do that again" is a reminder that these machines and hand tools do not forgive carelessness.

The reality is simple. Every tool in your shop, from the vise to the waterjet, has one thing in common. It does not care about you. It does not care if you are tired, distracted, or rushing to finish "just one more pass." It will do exactly what it is designed to do, and if you put yourself in the wrong place, it will treat you like material.

That does not mean tools are enemies. They are partners. They are powerful ones. But partnerships require respect. Respect keeps you working day after day, instead of explaining to an ER nurse why your belt grinder has bite marks in it.

Think of your shop as a cast of characters. The grinder is the hungry one. It is always ready to eat steel or fingers. The buffer is the silent one. It looks harmless until it launches your blade across the room. The forge is the loud one. It is a furnace with no sense of humor. The drill press is the sneaky one. A deceptively patient trap waiting for an unclamped blade to spin like a propeller. The lathe is the crazy one. Always ready to pull you in like a noodle and squeeze you out flat. Even the shop vac has a dark side, it is the sinister one. It wants to turn sparks into campfires at a moment's notice. These characters do not care about you. They are not out to get you on purpose, but they will not pause, hesitate, or give you a second chance. This section should not make you anxious around cutting tools. It is built to help you work with them confidently and safely by knowing exactly what each machine is capable of when things go wrong.

No matter the tool, most shop injuries come down to the same few causes: distraction, improvisation, overconfidence, fatigue, and poor setup.

- Distraction; looking away "just for a second."

- Improvisation; using the wrong tool because it was closer.

- Overconfidence; "I have done this a hundred times, nothing will happen."

- Fatigue; pushing through when you should rest.

- Poor setup; loose clamps, bad lighting, or rushed prep.

Your grinder isn't your friend. It's a hungry metal-eating demon that tolerates you.

Every maker who has been around long enough has their story. The grinder that ate a glove. The blade that launched out of a buffer. The file that stabbed a palm because it did not have a handle. Each story is a reminder that most injuries are not freak accidents. They are preventable.

Tool safety is not only about the "big" machines. Yes, presses, hammers, and grinders deserve fear. But many makers get hurt by the quiet tools: a slipping file, a broken sharpening stone, a jig that was not built quite right. The smaller the tool, the easier it is to underestimate it. And yet the cuts from sharpening accidents are often the deepest. The fires from polishing compounds are often the hardest to put out. The magnets, jigs, and fixtures that seem harmless can pinch, crush, or launch parts if treated casually. This section does not just cover the heavy hitters. It includes everything from grinders and buffers to sharpening systems and magnets. Because in the shop, the little details matter.

This section is written to help you respect the tools enough to use them wisely. That respect looks like wearing the right PPE for the right job, understanding the specific hazards of each tool, using proper setups, clamping, and workholding, reading the manuals, safety sheets, and instructions (yes, even for sharpening compounds), and recognizing that fatigue, rushing, and improvisation are enemies as dangerous as any spinning blade.

At the end of the day, the tools in your shop are what make your craft possible. They are the muscle, the precision, and the speed behind your work. But they are also the most common source of injuries, fires, and near misses. Respect them, use them well, and they will serve you for a lifetime. Take them for granted, and they will remind you why safety is written in scar tissue.

The lathe doesn't care how experienced you are. It still wants your sleeve.

Section 2.1 – Grinders & Sanders

The belt grinder is one of the single most important machines in a knifemaker's shop. It is the tool that turns raw stock into blades, shapes handles, and polishes edges. But it is also one of the more dangerous tools you will ever use. Unlike a forge or an anvil, the grinder has no rhythm, no warning glow, and no slow build-up. It moves at speed, keenly waiting for a mistake.

Almost every experienced maker has a grinder story. One recalls a snapped belt that lashed across his face, leaving a scar he sees in the mirror every morning. Another remembers freehand polishing a knife tip when it caught and launched across the room, burying itself in a wooden wall. More than one shop has burned down after sparks were pulled into a dust collector and smoldered unnoticed until midnight. These are not rare flukes. They are the natural consequences of underestimating a machine designed to chew through steel. The grinder does not discriminate between blade and body. It does not stop when a belt breaks. It does not forgive when a glove gets caught. The only real protection you have is a combination of habits, vigilance, and preparation.

This section does not aim to make you fearful of your grinder. It aims to make you respect it. Because when treated with respect, the grinder becomes a versatile, creative extension of your craft. Treated carelessly, it will take from you more than it gives.

Major Hazards

- Entanglement: loose sleeves, gloves, hair, or strings get pulled in instantly.
- Projectile Blades: weak grip, poor clamping, or catch points launch blades like missiles.
- Sparks & Dust: sparks ignite rags or bins; dust clouds damage lungs.
- Heat: overheated work burns hands and ruins temper.
- Kickback & Catch Points: gut hooks, serrations, or thin tips can snag and whip the blade violently.

PPE Reinforcement

- Eyes: always wear safety glasses and a face shield when grinding. Belts can and do break, and the slap comes too fast to dodge. Only layers of protection stand between you and blindness.
- Respiratory: a P100 respirator is required. Dust from G10, micarta, and exotic woods is invisible poison for your lungs.

  Hearing: grinders run at a scream. Without protection, hearing loss is guaranteed.
- Clothing: no gloves, no long sleeves, no dangling cords. A leather apron adds protection against sparks and belt slap.

> Saws cut wood. They also cut your fingers if you look away for half a second.

Safe Work Practices

- Work Position: stand square and focused. Do not rely on "dodging" failures. Protect yourself with PPE and awareness.

- Listen to the Belt: belts often warn before they fail. A rhythmic "tick" or off-beat slap is the splice loosening. Stop immediately and replace it.

- Clamping: use clamps or jigs for small or thin workpieces. Hands are not clamps.

- Backing Boards: essential for grinding gut hooks, tips, or details. They prevent snags.

- Tool Rests: use them whenever possible. Freehand grinding requires stability and experience.

- Control Pressure: let the abrasive do the cutting. Forcing steel into the belt increases the chance of grabbing, breaking, or launching.

Using the Right Tool Versus Being Creative

- Right Tool for the Job: choose belts, grits, and speeds wisely. Hogging steel with a polishing belt, or running hardened steel on a woodworking sander, is asking for failure.

- Safe Creativity: grinders are versatile. Shaping handles, polishing fittings, even grinding full convex bevels are all possible. Creativity is part of the craft. But respect physics. Ask yourself: "Could this catch, bind, or fling?" If yes, rethink it.

- Unsafe Creativity:
  - Running belts past their lifespan. They will snap.
  - Grinding on unsupported belt edges. Belts can tear sideways.
  - Forcing tiny pieces into a 2x72 without a jig. Your fingers will lose that fight.

Fire Prevention

- Place a spark guard or catch tray under the grinder.

- Never grind directly into a dust collector without a spark arrestor.

- Sweep and clear the grinder's surroundings daily.

- Keep an extinguisher within reach of your grinding station.

That cutoff wheel is one bad angle away from turning you into a lawn sprinkler.

Maintenance & Setup

- Belt Inspection: check every belt before use. If it sounds wrong, stop.

- Tracking: a properly tracked belt runs smoothly. A wandering belt is a danger.

- Wheel Health: cracked or loose wheels can fail explosively.

- Bearings & Platen: maintain tightness and smoothness. Vibration is both a safety risk and a quality killer.

Ergonomics, Posture & Fatigue

The grinder is not just dangerous when it is loud and fast. It is dangerous when you are tired, off-balance, or straining. Good posture and ergonomics do not just prevent back pain. They prevent accidents.

- Stance & Balance:
  - Stand with feet shoulder-width apart, knees slightly bent.
  - Keep your weight balanced, not leaning into the grinder. If you lose footing, you want to step back safely, not fall forward into the belt.
- Work Height: your grinder should be set so the platen is roughly at elbow height when standing. Too low equals hunching and fatigue. Too high equals bad leverage and loss of control.
- Support & Rest:
  - Rest your wrists or forearms on tool rests or work supports whenever possible. Stability reduces slips.
  - For long grinding sessions, alternate hands when possible to avoid fatigue on one side.
  - Micro-Breaks: grinding is physically and mentally tiring. Take short breaks to stretch, hydrate, and reset your posture. Fatigue slows reaction time, and the grinder only gives you fractions of a second to react.
- Lighting & Visibility: poor posture often comes from leaning in to see the work. Fix it with good lighting instead of contorting your body.
- Hearing Fatigue: long exposure to grinding noise causes not just hearing loss but also mental fatigue. Hearing protection reduces both.

Rule: if you are fighting the grinder, your body position is wrong. The tool should feel like an extension of your stance, not a tug-of-war.

The drill press is patient. It will wait until you're distracted, then take a
finger as payment.

Small Shop Notes

- Position grinders so sparks shoot into safe zones, not dust bins or flammable walls.

- Small benchtop grinders can hurt you just as badly as a 2x72. Do not dismiss them.

- If you lack proper dust collection, grind outdoors or use a portable HEPA hood.

Belt grinders don't have feelings, but they do have opinions about your knuckles.

Section 2.2 – Buffers & Polishers

The buffer is a very deceptively dangerous machine in the shop. To the untrained eye, it is just a motor with a soft cloth wheel spinning at speed. It is far less intimidating than the roar of a grinder or the fire of a forge. But ask any veteran knifemaker, and you will hear the same warning. The buffer is the tool that kills. Why? Because when a blade catches in a buffer, it does not just slip out of your hands. It is launched like a spear. The motor's power does not care if it is polishing steel or propelling it through your body.

There are sobering stories that illustrate this point. A respected knifemaker lost his life when a buffer caught a blade and hurled it into his chest. He was standing in the wrong zone, directly in line with the wheel's throw path. Another maker required reconstructive surgery after a guard fitting was ripped from his hands. The buffer spun it like a tornado and split his palm open. A third, buffing without a face shield, took a ricocheted part straight to the cheekbone. His glasses saved his eye, but the impact fractured his face. These are not rare freak accidents. They are common enough that entire generations of makers warn apprentices. Respect the buffer, or do not use it at all. Some makers even remove buffers from their shops entirely, choosing slower finishing methods over the risks.

This section is not here to scare you away from using the buffer. It is here to put the machine in its proper place. It is a powerful but merciless tool. If you use one, you must know its rules, its danger zones, and its habits. Used with respect, it gives a brilliant finish. Used carelessly, it becomes a lethal weapon.

Major Hazards

- Workpiece Launch: blades and fittings get caught and hurled at high speed.
- Entanglement: loose clothing, long hair, or gloves pulled into the wheel instantly.
- Kickback Zones: the "wrong" side of a wheel throws the workpiece directly at your body.
- Noise & Dust: less than grinders, but still a factor. Polishing compounds and cloth dust can irritate lungs.

PPE Reinforcement

- Eyes & Face: safety glasses plus a full face shield. A flying blade can destroy glasses alone.
- Respiratory: a dust mask or P100 respirator. Buffing compounds create fine airborne particles.
- Clothing: no gloves, no sleeves. Secure hair. Wear a heavy apron. It will not stop a blade, but it may deflect glancing impacts.
- Footwear: steel-toe boots. Dropped blades are still sharp.

The bandsaw is quiet… until it decides today is the day it eats your lunch.

Safe Work Practices

- Use the Safe Zone: always work on the lower front quadrant of the wheel. So if the wheel grabs, it throws the workpiece downward, away from you.

- Never Overreach: keep both hands firmly on the workpiece. If you cannot grip securely, clamp or jig it.

- Wheel Speed: use the slowest speed that still polishes effectively. Higher RPM's multiply danger.

- Workpiece Prep: avoid polishing unfinished or sharp-edged blades. Cover sharp edges with tape or backing boards when possible.

- Pressure Control: light, steady pressure. Forcing the blade into the wheel increases the chance of grab.

- No Distractions: buffing requires full attention. Answer the phone after the wheel stops.

Maintenance & Setup

- Wheel Condition: replace frayed, loose, or hardened wheels. Worn edges grab aggressively.

- Arbor Security: ensure wheels are tightened and balanced. A loose wheel can fly off.

- Guards & Shields: use wheel guards where possible. Many makers remove them, but they provide crucial protection.

- Keep Compound Fresh: do not overload wheels with dried, caked compound. It creates uneven grab.

Ergonomics & Fatigue

- Buffing requires steady control. Never use a buffer when tired, shaky, or rushed.

- Stand balanced, feet shoulder-width apart. Do not lean over the wheel.

- Work at elbow height if possible. Too low causes bending, too high weakens grip.

- Take breaks. Tension builds in shoulders and wrists. Fatigue makes slips inevitable.

Small Shop Notes

- If you do not absolutely need a buffer, do not use one. Safer finishing options exist (hand sanding, Scotch-Brite wheels, low-RPM polishers).

- If space is tight, ensure no one else is in line with your buffer's throw path.

- Use jigs for small parts. Never try to polish coin-sized fittings by hand.

Never trust a machine that's been running too smoothly. It is planning something.

Section 2.3 – Drill Presses & Drilling Safety

The drill press is one of the most common tools in the shop and one of the most underestimated. It does not roar like a chop saw or throw sparks like a plasma cutter, so it lulls many makers into a false sense of security. Do not be fooled. The drill press has torque, leverage, and patience. It does not need speed to injure you. It needs just one careless moment. A few hard-learned stories from real shops illustrate the point.

The propeller blade: a maker decided to "just hold" a knife tang while drilling pin holes. The bit grabbed, and the blade spun like a propeller, slashing his hand before he could react. He now clamps every piece without exception.

The flying chuck key: another maker left the chuck key in place when starting the machine. It shot across the shop like a bullet and buried itself in the drywall. A few inches in another direction, and it could have cost him an eye.

The glove trap: a hobbyist thought he was safe wearing gloves. The bit caught the fabric, winding it tight in seconds and twisting his fingers until bones broke.

The hidden edge: a knife clamped flat without a backing board left its sharpened edge exposed under the vice. While adjusting, the maker brushed against it and needed stitches.

Lesson: the drill press is not gentle. It is just quieter. Treat it with respect, clamp your work, and never forget that even a bench-top drill press can turn steel into a weapon.

Major Hazards

- Entanglement: loose sleeves, gloves, or long hair get pulled in instantly.
- Spinning Workpieces: unclamped stock becomes helicopter blades.
- Flying Bits: overloaded or dull bits snap and fling sharp shards.
- Pinch Points: fingers caught between bit, chuck, and workpiece.
- Noise & Chips: loud drilling and flying hot chips.
- Heat & Sparks: drilling hardened steel can throw sparks and generate extreme heat. It is enough to ignite oily rags nearby or cause burns.

> Your welder is not "just a little warm." It's one spark away from a light show you don't want.

PPE Reinforcement (Task-Specific)

Always: safety glasses are mandatory. Chips are sharp, hot, and unpredictable.

When Drilling Steel:

- Glasses plus face shield for added chip and spark protection.
- Hearing protection for large diameter bits or prolonged jobs.
- Cutting oil is not PPE, but it protects your workpiece and your bit.

When Drilling Hardened or Specialty Steels:

- Expect sparks and higher heat. Clear combustibles nearby and keep water or oil for cooling.
- Wear long sleeves made from natural fibers (cotton, leather) for burn protection. Synthetics can melt.

When Drilling Wood, G10, or Micarta:

- P100 respirator or dust mask. These materials create toxic dust and fine particulates.
- Eye protection is still required. Splinters and fibers are sharp.

Clothing:

- No gloves. Ever.
- Tie back long hair and sleeves.
- Remove jewelry. The press does not care if it is a wedding ring. It will take it anyway.

Safe Work Practices

- Clamping is mandatory: never hold your work by hand. If the bit grabs, clamps will resist, your hands do not.
- Backing Boards: protect bits, prevent wandering, and shield against exposed sharp edges.
- Use the Right Speed:
    - Small bits equal high speed.
    - Large bits equal slow speed.
    - Hardened steel equals slowest speed plus oil.
    - Refer to bit manufacturers recommendations if unsure about the right speeds.
- Step Drilling: drill large holes progressively. It prevents excessive heat, bit stress, and sudden grabs.
- Lubrication: use cutting oil on steel, wax on aluminum, water on titanium if necessary. It reduces sparks and heat.
- Clear Heat Hazards: no oily rags, solvents, or wood dust near drilling hardened steels.
- Hands Clear: keep fingers far from the clamp zone.
- Remove Chuck Key: immediately. Every time.

> Power tools don't have bad days. They just have days when they decide you do.

Bit Selection & Use

- High-Speed Steel (HSS): general-purpose. It works for mild steels, woods, and plastics. It is cheap but dulls quickly in hardened steel.

- Cobalt (M35/M42): stronger and heat-resistant. It is best for stainless and harder steels. It is more brittle, so clamp securely and do not side-load.

- Carbide: extremely hard and brittle. It is great for hardened steels or precision drilling. It will shatter under vibration. Always clamp securely.

- Step Bits: useful for thin stock or sheets. They are not for hardened steel. They overheat and grab.

- Sharpened Bits: dull bits equal heat, sparks, grabbing, and breakage. Keep them sharp or replace them.

Maintenance & Setup

- Bit Condition: replace or sharpen dull, chipped, or bent bits.

- Chuck Security: tighten properly, remove the key.

- Table Square: lock it in place. Crooked setups equal crooked holes and more grab.

- Belts & Pulleys: check condition. A snapped belt mid-drill is part whip, part heart attack.

- Clean Table: use a brush or magnet, not your hand, to clear chips.

Ergonomics & Fatigue

- Table Height: adjust for upright posture. Hunching equals poor visibility and slower reaction.

- Stance: balanced stance, feet flat. Do not lean into the bit.

- Clamps as Helpers: save your wrists and shoulders. Clamps never get tired.

- Micro-Breaks: step away during long drilling sessions. Fatigue multiplies mistakes.

  Troubleshooting Common Problems

1. Bit Gets Stuck

- Cause: drilling too fast, too much pressure, or dull bits.

- Response: stop immediately. Reverse the press if possible, or gently free it by hand after full stop. Danger: forcing the workpiece can turn it into a propeller.

2. Bit Breaks Off

- Cause: excessive side pressure, dull bits, hardened steel, or poor alignment.

- Response: stop drilling. Use pliers or a magnet — never fingers. Clamp before removal. Danger: broken bit edges are razor sharp, like tiny shards of glass.

That pile of oily rags isn't décor. It's a future bonfire with your name on it.

3. Excessive Heat, Smoke, or Sparks

- Cause: wrong speed, dull bit, no lubrication, hardened steel.

- Response: stop, let the bit cool, adjust speed, use proper lubrication, and keep combustibles away. Danger: overheated bits snap more easily, and sparks ignite nearby hazards.

4. Bit Wanders or Walks

- Cause: hard surface, no center punch, dull bit tip.

- Response: use center punch, drill pilot hole, sharpen or replace bit. Danger: wandering bits scratch blades or suddenly catch.

5. Chips Jam the Hole

- Cause: not clearing chips often enough, too much feed pressure.

- Response: back out often, clear chips with air or brush — never fingers. Danger: packed chips increase heat and binding.

Small Shop Notes

- Bench-top presses can be just as dangerous as floor presses. Torque does not care about size.

- Keep space clear around the drill press. Tripping mid-operation is a quick way to add blood to your project.

- Always have a small bin or magnet for chips. Brushing with your hand guarantees burns and splinters.

- Jigs and vises are worth it. Fingers are not holding fixtures.

Dust doesn't look dangerous until it's turning your lungs into sandpaper.

Section 2.4 – Cutting Tools: Band Saws, Chop Saws & Angle Grinders

Cutting tools are some of the more serious machines in the shop. They are the first step in transforming raw stock into usable material, and because of that they are used constantly. Band saws slice profiles, chop saws break down bar stock, and angle grinders cut or shape in ways no other tool can. Each of these machines gives you speed and efficiency. But they demand precision, awareness, and respect. Unlike grinders or buffers, cutting tools can feel approachable. The steady hum of a band saw, the quick chop of a cutoff saw, or the handheld convenience of an angle grinder make them seem like straightforward machines. But the dangers are very real. Every one of these tools has sharp teeth, spinning discs, or high-speed wheels that do not stop just because your hand slips or your material shifts.

The hazards come not only from the blades and wheels themselves, but from the way materials behave under them. Stock that is too small can be snatched away. Long bars can bind or whip if unsupported. Wood and composites can splinter without warning. Sparks from chop saws and grinders ignite dust or rags, and blades that are dull or poorly maintained are far more likely to break. Even the smallest band saw cut or angle grinder job can turn into an accident in a fraction of a second.This section is written to help you work with these cutting tools confidently and safely. Do not become timid or afraid because of what could go wrong. These guidelines will direct you to be able to use the tools safely and confidently. Proper blade selection, correct setup, the right PPE, and a habit of discipline are the dividing line between smooth shop work and a trip to the ER. As you read the subsections that follow, keep in mind one principle: cutting tools are never passive. They are always moving, always greedy, and always waiting for the smallest mistake. Respect them, and they will serve your craft faithfully. Forget their rules, and they will remind you, often painfully, that they are in charge.

Band Saws (Metal & Wood)

Band saws are quiet, versatile, and indispensable. But their quietness makes them deceptive. A moving blade does not care if it is cutting micarta, steel, or your hand.

Real stories:

- A dull blade broke mid-cut on micarta causing it to whip across a maker's forearm.
- A student rested his hand on the saw table while reaching for a drop. The stock slipped and his hand slid forward. The moving blade did its nasty work.
- Another resawing wood had the piece split unexpectedly, this pulled his fingers into the blade before he could pull away.

Recommendation: never rest your hand on the saw table while reaching down. Dust, oil, or smooth metal makes slipping into the blade dangerously easy.

Steel offcuts on the floor are just landmines for your feet.

Major Hazards

- Entanglement (loose clothing, hair, jewelry).
- Blade breakage from poor tension or dull teeth.
- Kickback from unsupported or twisted stock.
- Splinters and shards from micarta, G10, or hardwoods.

PPE Reinforcement (Task-Specific)

- Safety glasses. Face shields are recommended for brittle composites.
- P100 respirator for toxic dust.
- Ear protection for long sessions.
- Do not use gloves, use push sticks.

Safe Practices

- Use the correct blade for the material (fine-tooth for metal, coarse for wood).
- Keep hands clear of the cut path. Do not track with fingers.
- Always support long stock.
- Replace dull blades early, do not wait until they break.

Troubleshooting

- Blade wanders or cuts crooked: dull blade, low tension, or misaligned guides.
- Blade breaks: excessive pressure, wrong blade for material, or misalignment.
- Material burns or smokes: dull blade, wrong blade pitch, or feeding too fast.
- Work binds or kicks back: unsupported stock or twisting in the cut.

Chop Saws (Abrasive & Cold Cut)

Chop saws are fast and efficient, but unforgiving. Abrasive wheels shower sparks. Cold-cut saws kick hard if stock is not clamped. Real stories:

- Sparks from an abrasive wheel landed in oily rags. It caught on fire and spread before the operator noticed.
- Round bar, cut without clamping, rolled and launched like a spear across the shop, pinching fingers, and damaging property in the process.

> Magnesium doesn't need an invitation to ruin your day, it brings its own fireworks

Major Hazards

- Sparks igniting rags, solvents, or dust.
- Kickback from rolling or unsupported stock.
- Abrasive wheel shattering under stress.
- Intense noise and vibration.

PPE Reinforcement (Task-Specific)

- Safety glasses plus face shield.
- P100 respirator for abrasive dust.
- Ear protection always.
- Sturdy shoes.

Safe Practices

- Clamp all stock, especially round bars.
- Use wheels rated for your saw's RPM.
- Stand slightly aside, not in the wheel's path.
- Keep sparks away from combustibles.

  Troubleshooting
- Wheel binds: forcing stock or misalignment. Clamp correctly. Let the saw do the work.
- Wheel glazing (cuts slow): wheel worn smooth. Dress or replace.
- Excessive sparks: wrong wheel or dull wheel. Replace immediately.
- Wheel shatters: wrong speed rating, side-loading, or damage. Always inspect before use.

Oily rags don't spontaneously combust… they just get really enthusiastic about it.

Angle Grinders

The angle grinder is beloved for its versatility and feared for its violence. At 10,000 RPM, discs do not just break. They explode.

Real stories:

- A thin cutoff wheel shattered causing fragments to tear into a maker's face shield. Without it, he would have lost an eye.
- A grinder was left plugged in while on a maker's lap when he swapped discs. An inadvertent move caused it to start, cutting him deeply.Stitches were required.
- A grinder used without the side handle kicked back violently, slicing deep into muscle.

Major Hazards

- Discs shattering from side pressure or defects.
- Kickback when catching an edge.
- Sparks igniting nearby dust or rags.
- Loss of control without guard or handle.
- Extreme noise and toxic dust.

PPE Reinforcement (Task-Specific)

- Glasses plus face shield.
- P100 respirator (especially for G10 or micarta).
- Ear protection always.
- Gloves allowed, but tight-fitting only.
- Flame-resistant clothing.

Safe Practices

- Always use guard and side handles.
- Only use discs rated for the grinder's RPM.
- Never grind with the edge of a cutoff wheel.
- Let discs cut at their pace. Do not force.
- Unplug before changing discs.
- Only use the correct size wheel for the tool.

That "harmless" little scrap of steel will absolutely ruin your day when you step on it.

Troubleshooting

- Wheel chatters: worn arbor, loose disc, or improper seating. Stop and reset.

- Disc shatters: side pressure, wrong application, or over-speeding. Replace with correct disc type.

- Grinder kicks: angle too steep or forcing the tool. Lighten pressure.

- Sparks everywhere: cutting hardened steel, wrong disc, or over-speed. Re-evaluate setup.

Small Shop Notes (All Cutting Tools)

- Keep separate blades and wheels for wood and metal.

- Sweep dust and chips regularly. Piles are slip and fire hazards.

- Use roller stands for long stock, not your knee or hands.

Chemicals don't care that you're in a hurry. They'll still melt your face off.

Section 2.5 – Lathes & Turning Tools

Lathes have earned the title of "the king of machine tools" because of their ability to shape, bore, polish, and thread with precision. In the knife shop they are used for machining guards, fittings, pommels, threaded parts, and sometimes even exotic handle materials. Woodturning lathes allow makers to create perfectly round, balanced handles, spacers, and decorative details. But lathes, despite their elegance, are also among the most serious tools in the shop. They do not just spin. They pull, wrap, and fling. Unlike a grinder, which grinds only where you push the work, a lathe spins continuously. If you get caught, it will not stop until you do.

It is easy to underestimate a lathe because the motion looks calm and controlled. But the forces at work are relentless. A chuck spinning at 1,000 RPM can grab loose clothing or hair and wrap it in an instant. A poorly clamped part does not just drop. It launches at the speed of the chuck. Long, curly chips of steel look harmless, but they are razor-sharp spirals that slice skin like barbed wire. In woodturning, a hidden knot or crack can cause a piece to explode, sending shards flying across the shop. Many serious shop accidents involve lathes. Machinists have been pulled in by drawstrings, gloves, or sleeves. Makers have had parts launched at chest height because they skipped proper clamping. And woodturners have had bowls shatter with enough force to break face shields due to defects in the wood blanks.

The takeaway is simple: lathes are extraordinary machines that reward patience, precision, and respect. They demand that you bring your full attention and never let your guard down.

Major Hazards

- Entanglement: loose clothing, sleeves, hair, or gloves sucked into the chuck or work.

- Flying Workpieces: poorly clamped metal or wood parts eject violently.

- Tool Kickback: dull or improperly set tools dig in, kicking back or snapping.

- Sharp Chips: steel spirals and wood shavings are deceptively sharp.

- Impact & Shrapnel: cracked wood blanks can shatter, flinging fragments.

- Noise & Dust: long turning sessions produce dust, noise, and airborne hazards.

The shop floor isn't a storage area. It's a tripping hazard with extra steps.

PPE

- Always: safety glasses plus a full face shield. Lathes produce continuous flying debris.

- For Metals: hearing protection, snug clothing, and no gloves.

- For Woodturning: a P100 respirator. Wood dust is highly hazardous. Aprons help deflect chips but must be fitted with no loose ties.

Special Note: never wear jewelry, watches, or anything dangling. The lathe will find it.

Safe Practices

- Setup & Clamping: always seat work fully in the chuck, tailstock, or between centers. Tighten properly.

- Inspect Workpieces: check metal for cracks or imbalance. Check wood for knots, voids, or splits.

- Tool Positioning: keep cutting tools sharp, on the rest, and at proper angle. Never freehand.

- Clearance: rotate the chuck by hand before starting to ensure no interference.

- Chip Clearing: never grab spirals. Stop the lathe and use pliers or a hook.

- Stay Clear: stand to the side when starting a lathe. Do not stand in line with the chuck.

- Speed Control: use the lowest effective speed. Higher RPM increases risk of ejection and injury.

- Hands Off: never sand, polish, or touch work with bare hands. Even friction can pull you in or cause an injury.

Troubleshooting

- Work Vibrates or Wobbles: work not seated properly, imbalance, or incorrect speed. Stop and reset.

- Tool Chatters: dull tool, loose rest, or wrong height. Adjust and re-sharpen.

- Workpiece Slips: jaws not tightened or wrong clamping method. Reseat immediately.

- Chips Tangle Around Work: stop before clearing. Spirals are razor-sharp.

- Wood Splits or Breaks: blank had hidden voids, or speed and feed too aggressive. Always inspect blanks carefully.

Wood dust is nature's way of saying "breathe this and see what happens."

Woodturning Specific Safety

- Blank Preparation: inspect wood for cracks, knots, or defects before mounting. Glue or reject questionable stock.

- Tool Rest Positioning: keep tool rest close to the work (⅛–¼ inch gap). Adjust frequently as diameter changes.

- Chip Hazards: wood chips may look harmless, but splinters and fine dust are inhalation risks. Always wear a respirator.

- Sharp Edges: freshly turned handles or parts may have razor-sharp corners. Deburr or sand edges before handling.

- Shrapnel Risk: large blanks (like for hidden tang handles or guards) can explode if weak. Stand to the side until balance is confirmed.

Small Shop Notes

- Mini-lathes are just as dangerous as industrial ones. Smaller does not mean safer.

- Keep floor space around the lathe clear. Tripping nearby is catastrophic.

- Mount a shield or barrier if working in shared spaces. Flying parts do not respect shop boundaries.

- Keep a chip hook nearby. Never grab spirals bare-handed.

- For woodturners, invest in dust collection. Wood dust is as much a health hazard as metal shrapnel.

Scrap metal doesn't belong on the floor. It belongs in the scrap bin… or the ER.

Section 2.6 – Surface Grinders & Mills

Surface grinders and milling machines bring an unmatched level of precision into the knife shop. When you need flatness, squareness, or repeatable accuracy, these machines deliver results that handheld tools simply cannot. Knife makers use them to flatten bar stock, prepare tang shoulders, cut slots, machine guards, or ensure that two mating surfaces fit together perfectly. Precision tools also carry their own set of dangers. Unlike a grinder that sprays sparks or a saw that howls as it cuts, these machines can appear deceptively calm. A mill's cutter may spin smoothly, or a surface grinder's wheel may hum steadily until the moment something goes wrong. When it does, the result is sudden and violent. For example, a knifemaker setting up a surface grinder skipped cleaning the magnetic chuck. When his blade shifted under the pressure of the wheel, it launched sideways and buried itself in the shop wall. Another machinist underestimated the brittleness of carbide end mills. Under too much side load, the cutter snapped into multiple fragments, each traveling across the shop like miniature darts.

These machines do not tolerate improvisation. With surface grinders and mills, success comes from methodical preparation and respect for the process. If you cut corners, they will remind you. The reminder is fast, sharp, and usually expensive.

Major Hazards

- Workpiece Ejection: poor clamping or dirty magnetic chucks allow parts to slip or launch.

- Tool Breakage: end mills, cutters, and wheels snap under side pressure.

- Entanglement: loose clothing, hair, or gloves pulled into rotating cutters.

- Pinch/Crush Points: between table, vise, and fixtures.

- Sharp Chips & Dust: metal chips are razor sharp; abrasive dust damages lungs.

- Noise & Vibration: long sessions strain hearing and body.

PPE

- Safety glasses always; face shield strongly recommended.

- Hearing protection for extended runs.

- P100 respirator when grinding or cutting G10, micarta, or wood.

- Fitted clothing only; no gloves, no jewelry, no sleeves.

- Steel-toe boots protect against dropped stock.

Woodworking is just carving until the chisel decides it wants your thumb instead.

Safe Practices

- Setup is Everything: clean magnetic chuck or vise before clamping. Any dust or chips reduce holding strength.

- Clamping: use appropriate clamps, vises, or fixtures. Never hold stock by hand.

- Tool Selection: use the right wheel, cutter, or end mill for the material. Wrong tools break.

- Speed & Feed: respect recommended settings. Too fast overheats and breaks tools; too slow increases chatter.

- Coolant Use: use coolant or cutting fluid to reduce heat and prolong tool life.

- Hands Clear: keep hands off moving tables, wheels, and cutters.

- Stop Before Adjusting: never move stock, adjust clamps, or change tools with the spindle running.

Troubleshooting

- Workpiece Slips: chuck dirty or clamping insufficient. Stop, clean, and reset.

- Wheel Chatter: wheel out of balance, spindle misaligned, or incorrect feed rate. Dress or replace wheels.

- Tool Breaks: wrong tool for material, excessive side load, or improper speed. Switch to the correct cutter or reduce feed.

- Surface Burn Marks: too much heat, dull wheel, or no coolant. Dress wheel, reduce passes, use coolant.

- Chips Packing in Cut: not clearing chips. Use air blast, coolant, or clear manually when the machine is stopped.

Small Shop Notes

- Even small bench mills and surface grinders have enough power to launch parts. Treat them like full-size machines.

- Keep flammables away. Fine metal dust and sparks can ignite solvents and rags.

- For knife makers, smaller vises and fixtures make safer work than improvising with hand pressure.

- Mills and grinders are precision tools. Rushing only ruins parts and risks injury.

That beautiful exotic wood? It's also trying to give you an allergy attack.

Section 2.7 – Heat Treating Equipment (Forges & Electric Ovens)

Heat treating is the soul of bladesmithing. It is where steel transforms from raw stock into a hardened, functional blade. Forges, quench tanks, and electric ovens are the heart of this process, and they allow the maker to shape not only the blade's durability but also its character. Along with that power comes some of the most serious risks in the shop.

Unlike a grinder that chews steel in plain sight, or a drill press that roars when it grabs, the hazards of heat treating are often silent or hidden. Flames burn, gases leak, oils ignite, and carbon monoxide fills the air invisibly. Even more dangerous is how quickly familiarity breeds carelessness. The soft roar of a forge or the quiet glow of an oven can lull a smith into thinking everything is fine. Yet in the blink of an eye, a flare-up, an oil fire, or an unnoticed propane leak can escalate into disaster. And then there is the steel itself. Once the forge or heat-treat oven is lit, every piece of steel in the shop must be treated as hot until you check it. Heat treating is also where fire danger peaks. Propane or coal forges operate in the same spaces as quench tanks filled with oil, rags covered in grinding dust, and wooden benches. A single mistake. Dropping steel, splashing oil, or leaving equipment unattended can destroy both the work and the shop.

Real-world lessons: a bladesmith left a propane forge running unattended to grab a tool. The burner malfunctioned, and a small flame became a garage fire. Another quenched a hot blade in oil without a lid nearby. The oil ignited and flared chest-high, burning his arms and eyebrows.

Heat treating is where knife making feels most alive, but it is also where mistakes carry some of the steepest consequences. Respect the fire, respect the steel, and remember: you are working in an unforgiving part of the shop.

Forges

Major Hazards

- Burns: contact with hot steel, tongs, or forge lining.
- Fire: open flames, oil quenches, and hot scale can ignite rags or dust.
- Explosions: oil quench without ventilation, propane leaks, or water in quench oil.
- Toxic Fumes: burning coatings, coal smoke, scale dust, or superheated oils.
- Heat Stress: extended time near forges can cause dehydration and fatigue.

Epoxy is fun until it glues your fingers together like a bad prank.

PPE

- Safety glasses are mandatory at the forge.

- A face shield is beneficial during oil quenches or when handling large, sparking pieces.

- Heat-resistant gloves (short use only — do not rely on them for prolonged handling).

- Heavy natural-fiber or leather apron. Synthetics will melt.

- Closed-toe leather boots.

- P100 respirator for coal smoke, forge flux, or synthetic handle material fumes.

- Hearing protection if using forced-air burners or blowers.

Safe Practices

- Forge Placement: always forge in a well-ventilated, fire-safe area. Never in a closed room without exhaust.

- Propane Safety: check fittings for leaks with soapy water. Keep tanks outside, lines short, and shut off fuel when not in use.

- Coal/Charcoal Safety: ventilate for carbon monoxide. Keep detectors installed.

- Quenching Safety:

  - Use only oils rated for heat treating (Parks 50, AAA, etc.). Never motor oil. Motor oil smokes, ignites easily, and produces toxic fumes.

  - Use a deep, stable tank with a lid.

  - Always quench slowly and deliberately. Never drop steel.

  - Keep water away from oil quench tanks. Water plus oil equals explosion.

- Handling Hot Steel:

  - Every piece of steel in the shop is considered hot when the forge is on.

  - Dedicate a safe hot rack for resting blades.

  - Hover the back of your hand near the steel, then tap quickly with the back of your hand before picking it up.

- Cooling: let parts air cool on fireproof surfaces. Never leave them on wood benches.

Sanding seems harmless until you realize you've been breathing your project.

Electric Heat-Treat Ovens

Major Hazards

- Burns: handling hot steel, racks, or quench plates straight out of the oven.

- Electrical Risks: poor wiring, undersized circuits, or faulty cords can overheat and cause fires.

- Fire Hazards: hot scale or nearby combustibles too close to the oven.

- Heat Stress: extended operation in small rooms raises ambient shop temperature.

PPE

- Safety glasses are mandatory.

- Heat-resistant gloves when removing parts.

- Face shield recommended if handling multiple pieces or quench plates.

- Leather apron or heavy natural-fiber clothing.

- Closed-toe leather boots.

Safe Practices

- Electrical Setup:

  o Always run ovens on a properly rated breaker and wiring.

  o Avoid extension cords. They overheat easily under oven load.

  o Have wiring inspected if in doubt.

- Placement: keep ovens on fireproof stands with clear space around them. Do not push against walls.

- Operation:

  o Never overload with steel beyond rated capacity.

  o Do not open the door repeatedly mid-cycle. Heat shock can damage both steel and elements.

- Handling Steel: use tongs or holders to remove parts. Place on fireproof trays or quench plates immediately. Keep quench plates or tanks close to the oven to avoid carrying glowing steel across the shop.

Troubleshooting

- Oven Trips Breaker: circuit overloaded or wiring undersized. Use a proper dedicated circuit.

- Uneven Heat Zones: load too large, thermocouple failing, or poor placement of steel. Rotate or reduce load.

- Element Failure: age, overheating, or contamination. Replace promptly. Do not run on weak elements.

- Oven Will Not Hold Temperature: check controller, thermocouple, and electrical connections.

- Smoke from Oven: oils, coatings, or contaminants burning off. Improve ventilation, clean steel before heat treat.

Small Shop Notes

- Store propane cylinders outside, upright, away from heat.

- Keep at least two fire extinguishers in the shop. One near the forge, one at the exit.

- Never leave a forge or oven unattended. Heat treating is not a walk-away process.

- Install carbon monoxide detectors in every forging area.

- Keep a burn kit handy. Not just a first aid kit.

- Use a surge protector or line conditioner for ovens in areas with unstable power.

Section 2.8 – Welding & Hot Work

Hot work is any process that uses heat, flame, or sparks to cut, shape, or join metal. In the knife shop this can include welding (stick, MIG, TIG), oxy-acetylene torches, plasma cutting, brazing, and even simple soldering. While these techniques are not always part of knife making itself, they become essential for building jigs, repairing tools, modifying equipment, or fabricating parts of your shop setup. Many knife makers eventually find themselves behind a welding hood or torch, even if they did not plan on it. But hot work comes with some treacherous risks in the shop: blinding light, molten metal, compressed gas, explosive sparks, and toxic fumes. Unlike grinders or saws, which mostly threaten your fingers and arms, hot work can injure your whole body in one mistake. Welders suffer from eye damage, plasma cutters can set shops ablaze, torches can leak or explode, and brazing or soldering without ventilation can poison your lungs.

Real-world lessons show how quickly things can go wrong. A maker welding a stand in shorts caught a ball of slag in his lap. The burns took months to heal. Another forgot to check his oxygen/acetylene torch fittings. A slow leak filled his garage with gas, and when he struck a spark the explosion took out windows and set the wall ablaze. A plasma cutter user neglected ventilation. Cutting galvanized steel gave him metal fume fever that landed him in the ER.

Hot work gives you tremendous freedom, but it comes with serious responsibility. Every flame, spark, or arc is a potential fire, and every joint you weld or cut exposes you to hidden hazards. The rest of this section breaks down the major processes, their risks, and how to stay safe while using them.

Arc, MIG, & TIG Welding

Major Hazards

- Arc Flash: UV light causes welder's flash, painful burns to the eyes and skin.

- Molten Spatter: hot metal balls can roll into boots, laps, or pockets.

- Electric Shock: faulty grounding or wet conditions can kill instantly.

- Fumes: galvanized, stainless, and flux-cored welding create toxic vapors.

- Fire: sparks and slag ignite dust, rags, or solvents.

Glue fumes don't make you high. They just make you stupid.

PPE

- Welding helmet with proper shade lens.

- Flame-resistant jacket and gauntlet gloves.

- Safety boots (no mesh tops).

- Respirator for fumes (especially stainless, galvanized, or indoors).

- Ear protection for long runs or confined spaces.

Safe Practices

- Always ground the welder properly.

- Keep your work area dry. Never weld in wet shoes or on damp floors.

- Remove combustibles from the welding area.

- Ventilate or use fume extraction.

- Cover skin. Arc flash burns feel like sunburn but come faster and worse.

Troubleshooting

- Porous Welds: contaminated base metal, damp rods, or poor gas flow.

- Arc Sticking (Stick Welding): wrong amperage or rod angle.

- Excessive Spatter: too high amperage, wrong polarity, or poor shielding gas.

Oxy-Acetylene Torch

Major Hazards

- Gas Leaks: unchecked fittings can fill the shop with explosive gas.

- Flashback: flame burns back into the hose, risking cylinder explosion.

- Burns: torches produce invisible heat beyond the flame tip.

- Cylinder Hazards: acetylene above 15 psi is unstable and explosive.

Finishing chemicals are like that friend who seems nice until they burn your skin off.

PPE

- Shaded goggles (minimum shade 5 for cutting).

- Flame-resistant gloves and jacket.

- Boots, no cuffs that catch sparks.

- A heavy leather apron is recommended.

Safe Practices

- Check all hoses and fittings with soapy water before lighting.

- Purge lines before use.

- Open acetylene slowly. Never exceed 15 psi.

- Light acetylene first, then add oxygen.

- Store tanks upright, chained, with caps on.

Troubleshooting

- Popping Flame: torch tip dirty or wrong oxygen/acetylene balance.

- Backfire/Flashback: check for clogged tip, low gas pressure, or missing flashback arrestor.

Plasma Cutting

Major Hazards

- UV & Infrared Flash: same danger as welding. It burns eyes and skin.

- Molten Sparks: spray in all directions, often farther than you expect.

- Toxic Fumes: especially from galvanized or coated steels.

- Electrical Hazards: poor grounding or damaged leads.

Sharp tools are better than dull ones. Until you find out how sharp they really are.

PPE

- Plasma-rated helmet or shield.
- Flame-resistant gloves and jacket.
- Respirator for fumes.
- Safety boots.
- A heavy leather apron is recommended.

Safe Practices

- Ground the work properly before cutting.
- Clear a large spark zone. Plasma throws fireballs 10+ feet.
- Ventilate aggressively, especially indoors.
- Replace worn consumables before they fail mid-cut.

Troubleshooting

- Rough Cuts: worn nozzle, wrong amperage, or moving too fast.
- No Arc Start: bad ground, failed electrode, or loose connection.
- Excessive Dross: cutting too slowly or wrong torch angle.

Brazing & Soldering

Major Hazards

- Fumes: fluxes and metals release harmful vapors.
- Burns: torches, soldering irons, and hot metal all burn instantly.
- Lead Exposure: old solders may contain lead. Avoid it entirely.
- Fire: open flames ignite nearby dust or rags.

Band-aids are not a personality trait. They're a warning sign.

PPE

- Safety glasses.

- Gloves resistant to heat.

- Respirator for flux fumes.

Safe Practices

- Clean all joints thoroughly before heating.

- Use the correct flux and filler for the metals.

- Ventilate workspaces. Flux smoke builds up quickly.

- Cool parts on fireproof surfaces.

Troubleshooting

- Poor Flow: base metal not clean, wrong flux, or insufficient heat.

- Weak Joint: wrong filler alloy or overheating burned out the flux.

Practical Shop Notes

- Store gas cylinders upright, chained, with caps on.

- Keep welding separate from dust collection areas. Sparks plus dust equals fire.

- Always ventilate. Welding and brazing fumes are cumulative health hazards.

- Maintain a fire watch after welding or cutting. Embers can smolder for hours.

- Never weld or cut on sealed containers. They can explode violently.

A tourniquet is a terrible fashion accessory, but a great last resort.

Section 2.9 – Hydraulic Presses & Power Hammers

Presses and power hammers are the heavy hitters of the forging world. Where grinders refine and mills measure, these machines move steel in dramatic ways. A hydraulic press applies a slow, unstoppable force. It is capable of crushing billets into shape, consolidating Damascus, or pressing fittings with precision. A power hammer, by contrast, delivers rapid-fire blows, imitating a blacksmith's arm but with the strength of an army. Both machines serve the same purpose. They take the burden of heavy forging away from the smith's body and place it on a machine. With them, work that once took hours of swinging a hammer can be done in minutes. They are, in many ways, what allows modern bladesmiths to tackle projects that would have been impossible in a purely hand-forged shop. With this power comes serious risk. A hydraulic press does not care whether it is squeezing a billet of Damascus or your fingers. It moves with quiet inevitability, and once it starts, it rarely stops in time to spare mistakes. A power hammer, on the other hand, is loud, violent, and relentless. It does not politely pause when you fumble. It keeps smashing, and whatever is under its dies will be struck, whether steel, tong, or hand.

Real-world lessons show how quickly things can go wrong. A bladesmith using a hydraulic press ignored a small hydraulic leak. The line burst under pressure, spraying fluid onto hot steel and igniting a flash fire. Another was adjusting dies on a running power hammer. A mistimed reach crushed his glove flat against hot metal. He was lucky to keep his hand. More than one maker has underestimated vibration and foundation needs. A poorly anchored hammer has walked across the shop floor while running. What makes these tools especially threatening is the false sense of security they can create. Presses move slowly, giving the illusion of safety. But that force is enough to turn steel into pancakes, and skin and bone do not stand a chance. Power hammers, by contrast, are so fast and violent that many operators think of them as too wild to control. But with the right foundation, rhythm, and respect, they can be remarkably precise.

Both machines are indispensable in a forging shop. They are safe only if you treat them with the awareness that they will never forgive distraction or complacency.

Major Hazards

- Crush Points: dies and rams exert massive force.

- Hydraulic Failures: hose bursts, leaks, and high-pressure fluid injection.

- Flying Debris: scale or billets ejecting under pressure.

- Noise & Vibration: long-term hearing loss, shop fatigue, and equipment damage.

- Hot Work Hazards: working billets can eject hot scale or even split violently.

- Foundation Risks: unanchored power hammers can move or topple

That little cut? It's just waiting to get infected and ruin your week.

PPE

- Safety glasses mandatory; face shield recommended.
- Hearing protection (earmuffs strongly advised).
- Heavy gloves for handling billets. But never around moving dies.
- Steel-toe boots to guard against dropped billets.
- Natural-fiber clothing or leather apron.

Safe Practices

Machine Setup:

- Ensure presses and hammers are properly anchored to foundations.
- Inspect dies for cracks or damage before use.
- For presses: check hydraulic lines, fittings, and fluid levels regularly.

Operation:

- Never place hands or tools between dies while powered.
- Use tongs or long-handled tools for billet placement.
- Keep bystanders at a safe distance. Scale ejects unpredictably.
- On power hammers, establish rhythm before approaching steel.

Hydraulic Safety:

- Address leaks immediately. High-pressure fluid can penetrate skin.
- Use only rated hoses and fittings.
- Keep flammables away from the press area.

Shutdown & Maintenance:

- Always power down and depressurize before adjusting dies.
- Lubricate moving parts on hammers regularly to prevent seizing.
- Maintain proper oil levels and filtration in presses.

Eye wash is for when you realize "I'll be fine" was a lie.

Troubleshooting

- Press Loses Power: check fluid levels, leaks, or failing pumps.

- Jerky Motion (Press): air in hydraulic system or worn seals.

- Excessive Vibration (Hammer): poor foundation, loose bolts, or uneven dies.

- Unstable Operation (Hammer): worn bearings, poor lubrication, or misaligned dies.

- Scale Ejecting Excessively: reduce force per strike, improve billet prep, wear full PPE.

Practical Shop Notes

- Always keep presses and hammers on proper foundations.

- Never weld or modify dies without checking alignment and fit.

- Keep a clear zone around machines. Billets can eject unpredictably.

- Maintain hearing protection. Prolonged use leads to permanent damage.

- Schedule regular inspections of hydraulics and lubrication systems.

Burn gel is cheaper than skin grafts. Use it.

Section 2.10 – Shop Vises, Clamps, & Workholding

The vise and the clamp are the quiet guardians of the shop. They do not roar, spark, or smash steel, but they quietly make every other tool safer. No matter how good your grinder, saw, or drill press is, if the workpiece is not secured, the job instantly becomes dangerous. Proper workholding is the difference between a clean operation and a trip to the ER.

Vises, clamps, and fixtures act as the third hand every maker wishes they had. They let you put steel exactly where you need it and keep it there, steady and predictable. They protect your actual hands by keeping them out of the line of fire. But because they are so simple, they are often underestimated. A vise jaw loosens, a clamp slips, or a jig is not square, and suddenly a spinning drill bit or a moving saw is controlling the work instead of you. Unlike a grinder or hammer, which makes its danger obvious through sparks and noise, bad workholding fails quietly. A blade that looks secure in the vise can still shift under pressure. A clamp that looks snug might spring loose the second vibration sets in. And when it happens, steel does not politely stay in place. It launches, spins, or bites the nearest hand. Workholding is not limited to vises and clamps. Jigs, sleds, and push sticks are also workholding devices, especially on tools like table saws or band saws. Holding material freehand on these machines is one of the fastest ways to experience kickback, where the blade throws material back at you with violent force. Proper jigs and clamps not only keep your hands out of the blade's path, they also ensure accuracy and repeatability.

Real-world lessons show the consequences of poor workholding. A knifemaker left a blade clamped upright in a vise with no guard. While turning around, he walked straight into the exposed edge. Another drilled pin holes in a blade without clamping it properly. When the bit grabbed, the blade spun like a propeller and cut across his knuckles.

Workholding tools are the backbone of safe shop practice. They may not feel as exciting as a new grinder, but every time you skip clamping or cut corners on securing your work, you gamble with your hands, eyes, and safety.

Major Hazards

- Slips & Shifts: poor clamping allows workpieces to move unexpectedly.

- Kickback & Spin: unclamped blades or bars catch in drills or saws and spin violently.

- Pinch Points: fingers caught between jaws, clamps, or dropped parts.

- Blade Exposure: leaving sharp work clamped without covering edges.

- Clamp Failure: cheap or worn clamps can spring loose under load.

The shop's first-aid kit isn't a decoration. It's insurance.

PPE

- Safety glasses always. Chips fly when pieces shift.

- Hearing protection if using workholding with noisy tools.

- Gloves only when handling raw stock. Not when operating rotating machines nearby.

- Steel-toe boots for dropped clamps, vises, or heavy workpieces.

Safe Practices

- Clamping for Drilling: always clamp blades flat when drilling holes. Never hand-hold a blade under a drill press.

- Backing Boards: use wooden backing boards to prevent drill blowout and to cover sharp edges.

- Blade Protection: cover edges with wood, tape, or guards when clamped upright in a vise.

- Clamp Quality: invest in heavy-duty clamps rated for the task. Cheap ones break at the worst time.

- Workpiece Positioning:

  o Keep clamps clear of tool paths.

  o When using table saws or band saws, never hold material freehand. Always use a push stick, sled, or jig.

  o Offset body position slightly when working near spinning tools to avoid being in the direct path of kickback.

- Routine Check: tighten clamps after first operation. Vibration loosens everything.

Troubleshooting

- Workpiece Slips: clamp not tight, jaws oily, or not enough clamping force. Clean jaws, use pads, or switch to heavier clamps.

- Clamp Springs Loose: worn threads or poor quality. Replace immediately.

- Blade Shifts in Vise: add soft jaws, leather padding, or backing board.

- Stock Vibrates While Cutting: add secondary clamp or reposition closer to the cut.

- Practical Shop Notes

  Always keep spare clamps handy. Running out leads to cutting corners.

- Mark or color-code clamps for light versus heavy-duty use.

- Cover sharp edges in vises. It is easy to forget they are there.

- Inspect vises regularly for cracked jaws, loose bolts, or stripped threads.

Remember: vibration will loosen everything over time. Always re-check clamps mid-job.

"It's just a scratch" is what people say right before they need stitches.

Section 2.11 – Pneumatic Tools & Air Systems

Compressed air is one of the quiet workhorses of the shop. It does not get the attention of forges or grinders, but it powers a wide range of tools: die profilers for precision shaping, air chisels for rough cutting, sanders and grinders for finishing, even spray guns for coatings and sealants. For some makers, a sandblaster hooked up to a compressor is just as essential as a belt grinder. Pneumatics offer speed, versatility, and efficiency, often in a smaller, lighter package than their electric equivalents. Yet because they seem less dramatic, pneumatics often get treated casually. Many smiths think of compressed air as just air, forgetting that it is air under pressure. It is stored energy that can fail catastrophically. A cracked hose does not just leak. It whips violently like a bullwhip when broken. A rusted compressor tank does not just fail. It explodes with the force of shrapnel. Even small tools like die profilers or air chisels can send bits of steel flying, damage hearing, or wear out your hands with vibration. The hazards are not limited to the hardware. Sandblasting can destroy lungs if proper respirators are not worn. Paint and coating sprayers can fill a room with toxic mist in minutes. And one of the most overlooked risks is using compressed air to blow off dust from clothing or skin. This can inject air under the skin or even into the bloodstream, with potentially fatal results.

Real-world lessons show how dangerous misuse can be. A maker used an old air hose with cracked fittings. It burst under pressure, whipping across his arm and leaving deep welts. Another ran an air hammer all day without hearing protection. Years later, the ringing in his ears never stopped. A sandblaster operator failed to wear a respirator while using silica sand. Within weeks, he developed a serious respiratory illness. A hobbyist thought it was harmless to clean dust off his shirt with compressed air. The jet drove dust into a small cut, leading to a painful infection.

Compressed air tools are invaluable in the knife shop. They can speed up shaping, cleaning, and finishing, or clean a surface. But like every other tool here, they demand respect. Think of compressed air as invisible muscle: powerful, reliable, but unforgiving when misused.

Call 911 faster than you call your buddy to brag about the injury.

Major Hazards

- Hose Whip: burst or disconnected lines whip violently.
- Overpressure: tanks or tools failing from excessive PSI.
- Flying Debris: die profilers, air chisels, grinders, and sandblasters eject particles at high velocity.
- Noise Exposure: pneumatic hammers, chisels, and grinders exceed safe decibel levels.
- Air Injection: compressed air forced under skin or into the bloodstream.
- Dust & Fumes: sandblasting and spraying create severe respiratory hazards.
- Tank Failure: rust, poor maintenance, or improper draining can cause explosions.

PPE

- Safety glasses or face shield always, especially with blasting or grinding.
- Hearing protection for any prolonged use.
- Respirator for blasting, spraying, or dusty conditions.
- Gloves to protect against hose whip and vibration.
- Steel-toe boots for handling heavy tanks and equipment.

Safe Practices

- Air Supply
  - Never exceed rated PSI for hoses, tools, or tanks.
  - Drain compressor tanks daily to prevent rust and water buildup.
  - Install safety valves and regulators.
- Hose Management
  - Inspect hoses before use for cracks, leaks, or weak fittings.
  - Secure hoses and keep them clear of walkways to prevent tripping.
  - Always shut off air before disconnecting tools.
- Die Profilers
  - Keep work clamped securely. Profilers walk if not properly guided.
  - Use light, controlled strokes. Forcing the tool leads to broken bits.
  - Wear eye protection. Profiler tips can snap suddenly.

> Pain is your body's way of saying "you should have listened to the book."

- Air Chisels & Hammers
    - Always hold with two hands when possible.
    - Direct the chisel away from your body. They can slip on hardened material.
    - Never run without the proper retainer. Bits can launch like spears.
    - Use hearing protection. These are some of the loudest shop tools.
- Air Sanders & Grinders
    - Ensure sanding discs and grinding wheels are rated for air RPMs. They often spin faster than electric tools.
    - Check backing pads before every use. Worn pads can disintegrate at speed.
    - Never run grinders without guards in place.
    - Maintain a firm grip. Air grinders torque hard on startup.
    - Limit exposure. Vibration causes fatigue and long-term nerve damage (white finger).
- Sandblasters
    - Always blast inside a cabinet or proper booth.
    - Never use silica sand. Use approved media only.
    - Wear full PPE: blast hood or face shield, respirator, gloves.
    - Keep hoses short and secured to prevent whip.
- Spray Guns & Coating Tools
    - Use only in well-ventilated or exhausted areas.
    - Wear respirators designed for organic vapors, not just dust.
    - Ground equipment to prevent static discharge in flammable atmospheres.
    - Never spray near ignition sources. Many coatings are highly flammable.

Storage & Maintenance

- Keep compressors in ventilated areas.
- Replace worn hoses immediately. Do not tape over cracks.
- Ensure tanks are certified and inspected as required.

Super glue is for models, not for closing wounds… but we've all done it.

Troubleshooting

- Air Tool Lacks Power: low pressure, leaks, or clogged filters. Check regulator and lines.

- Compressor Overheating: overuse, blocked airflow, or low oil in lubricated units.

- Hose Whip on Disconnect: use quick-release fittings with safety locks.

- Moisture in Lines: drain tanks, add dryer or separator.

- Excessive Noise: faulty mufflers or worn tool bearings.

Practical Shop Notes

- Always bleed off pressure before servicing tools or lines.

- Never exceed 30 PSI for cleaning workpieces. Use OSHA-approved air nozzles.

- Label compressors with max working pressure.

- Mount compressors on vibration pads to reduce fatigue and noise.

- Keep dedicated respirators for blasting and spraying. Do not cross-use dusty respirators with clean jobs.

Electricity doesn't care that you're "pretty sure it's off."

Section 2.12 – Hand Tools & Anvils (Hammers, Files, Punches, Tongs, etc.)

Before the power tools, before the press, before the grinder there were hand tools. The hammer, the file, the punch, the anvil, and the tong are the oldest and most reliable instruments in any smith's shop. They require no electricity, no compressor, and no software update. They are simple, but they can still injure as quickly and permanently as any machine. Because they are quiet, hand tools are often underestimated. Swinging a hammer feels straightforward until vibration damage sets in after years of misuse. Filing seems safe until a sharp edge snaps and gouges a palm. Even the anvil, often treated like an indestructible piece of shop furniture, has its dangers. Striking at the wrong angle can send shards of scale into your face, and working your steel improperly on hardy tools can cause it to lurch awkwardly. And then there are tongs. They are meant to hold hot material, but they are capable of slipping, rotating, pinching, and heating up faster than you expect.

Real-world lessons show how quickly hand tools can cause injury. A smith used a file without a handle. When the tang slipped, it drove straight into his palm. Another swung a hammer all day on a poor stand. Years later, he struggled with wrist and elbow injuries from constant vibration. A maker rested a bar poorly while using a hardy tool and struck hard. The work popped free and flew across the shop like a spear. A beginner grabbed hot steel with oversized tongs. The jaws rotated, twisting the billet out of control, and left burn marks where the reins had heated up.

Hand tools are safe only when used with respect, patience, and proper technique. They may be ancient, but they still demand modern attention.

Major Hazards

- Impact Injuries: missed hammer blows striking hands or legs.
- Flying Scale/Chips: hammer strikes on hot steel or anvil edges.
- Vibration Damage: long-term white finger or joint strain from poor technique.
- Sharp Edges: files, chisels, and punches break or slip.
- Anvil Hazards: work slipping off hardy tools, rebound throwing steel, unstable stands.
- Tong Hazards: slipping jaws, oversized grip causing rotation, reins heating rapidly.

That extension cord is one frayed wire away from a light show.

PPE

- Safety glasses at all times.

- Hearing protection when hammering for extended sessions.

- Gloves optional for hammers and files.

- For tongs: rely on proper tong length, not gloves, to manage heat. Gloves may be worn for comfort, but not as a substitute for correct tong design.

- Steel-toe boots in case of dropped tools or hot workpieces.

- Natural-fiber clothing. Sparks and scale still fly.

Safe Practices

Hammers

- Choose the right hammer weight. Fatigue leads to sloppy strikes.

- Keep handles smooth, tight, and crack-free.

- Strike squarely. Avoid glancing blows that can chip steel or send work flying.

Files

- Always use a handle. Never grip a bare tang.

- Clamp material securely before filing.

- Keep files clean with a file card to prevent slipping.

Punches & Chisels

- Dress mushroomed heads regularly. Chips from hardened edges can fly into eyes.

- Strike only with a hammer appropriate for the tool.

- Use holders or tongs for hot work punches.

Grounding is not optional. It's what keeps you from becoming the ground.

Anvils

- Mount on a stable stand, secured from movement.

- Never strike directly on edges. Chips can fly.

- Keep the face clean and dry. Rust pits create weak spots in forging.

- When using hardy tools (hot cuts, swages, etc.), always secure your stock firmly. Poor placement leads to slipping or launching.

Tongs

- Use the right size tongs for the stock. Undersized jaws slip, oversized jaws rotate or drop steel unexpectedly.

- Tongs should have reins long enough to be used bare-handed. If you need gloves just to avoid heat transfer, your tongs are too short or poorly designed.

- Expect tong jaws to heat quickly when in contact with hot stock. Avoid prolonged holding over the forge.

- Store in a tong rack by stock size/type, not in piles. A wrong grab in a hurry can mean poor fit and lost control.

Troubleshooting

- Loose Hammer Head: wedge or re-handle immediately. Do not just finish the job.

- File Slips Often: work is not clamped or the file is clogged. Clean or chalk before use.

- Punch Mushrooming: grind smooth and re-shape. Do not wait for it to chip.

- Anvil Walking: poor stand or uneven floor. Shim or anchor.

- Tongs Lose Grip: jaws mismatched to stock, oversized reins, or bent alignment. Re-forge or replace.

  Practical Shop Notes

- Store hammers, files, and tongs off the floor. Rust and chips spread fast.

- Keep extra file handles ready. You will need them.

- Regularly resurface and dress punches, chisels, and anvils.

- Mount anvils at the right height. Knuckles when standing straight.

- Rotate hammer hands during long sessions to prevent repetitive strain.

- Keep a rack for tongs sized by stock dimension. Close enough grips are not safe.

Your shop vacuum is not a fan. It's a fire starter with a hose.

Section 2.13 – Specialty Machinery (Waterjets, CNC, EDM, Routers, Lasers, etc.)

Not every small knife shop has a waterjet, CNC router, EDM machine, or laser cutter. But these tools are showing up more and more in the world of custom making. Some makers buy desktop CNCs or hobby lasers. Others rely on community shops, makerspaces, or outsourcing to fabricators. Even if you do not own one, chances are you will use a part cut, slotted, or engraved by one of these machines sooner or later. Knowing their risks helps you make safer choices in how you design, order, or run work. Precision does not mean safety. A waterjet does not just cut steel. At 60,000 plus PSI, it will slice through flesh and bone in an instant. CNC machines spin cutters faster than the eye can follow, and a loose blank becomes a projectile with the speed and energy of a bullet. EDM machines operate with electricity and dielectric fluids. It is a recipe for fire if the wrong fluid is used. And lasers carry a double risk: invisible beams that can blind permanently in fractions of a second, as well as toxic fumes released when they cut plastics or composites. Because they often run in the background, it is tempting to treat them as safer than the roaring forge or the screaming grinder. But their hazards are quieter, more technical, and in some ways more dangerous because they are less obvious. Fires can start inside a laser cabinet in seconds. A CNC spindle will not stop just because you hesitated before reaching in. A waterjet does not care whether it is erasing titanium or your finger.

These machines are powerful allies for the modern maker. But they are also unforgiving. The best way to use them safely is to treat them not as background tools, but as machines every bit as dangerous as the forge or grinder, only in different subtler ways.

Major Hazards

- Waterjets: 60,000 plus PSI streams, abrasive splashback, noise.

- CNC Mills & Routers: flying cutters or workpieces, entanglement, high noise.

- EDM Machines: fire hazard from dielectric fluids, electrical risks.

- Laser Cutters/Engravers: eye damage from invisible beams, toxic fumes from plastics or composites, ignition of flammable materials.

General Hazards: unattended operation, coolant leaks, sharp chips and swarf, pinch points.

Wet hands and electricity go together like… well, they don't.

PPE

- Safety glasses or face shield for all chip-producing operations.

- Hearing protection for routers, CNCs, or waterjets.

- Laser safety glasses matched to your machine's wavelength. Not generic safety glasses.

- Gloves never near spindles or cutters. Handle chips with pliers or brushes instead.

- Respirator or fume extraction for engraving plastics, composites, or organics.

- Protective footwear for dropped blanks or machine fixtures.

Safe Practices

- Waterjets

  - Never open cabinet doors while running.

  - Treat the jet as live until fully depressurized.

  - Secure material completely to prevent deflection.

  - Handle abrasives carefully. Silica-based media is a respiratory hazard.

- CNC Mills & Routers

  - Always secure stock with proper fixturing (clamps, vises, vacuum tables).

  - Never reach into the machine while spindles are turning.

  - Use enclosures or shields to contain flying debris.

  - Do not run machines unattended unless designed for continuous manufacturing.

- EDM Machines

  - Use only approved dielectric fluids.

  - Maintain fire suppression nearby.

  - Keep electrical systems inspected and grounded.

- Laser Cutters/Engravers

  - Always use proper fume extraction or filtering.

  - Never look directly at the beam. Even reflections can cause permanent damage.

  - Never cut PVC, fiberglass, or unknown plastics. They release chlorine gas or carcinogens.

  - Stay nearby during operation. Fires can start suddenly.

Breakers are there for a reason. Ignoring them is how you become a cautionary tale.

- General

    o   Keep hands away from tool changers, moving spindles, and optics.

    o   Use chip brushes, not compressed air, to clear swarf.

    o   Keep floors clean and dry. Coolant and oil spills are slip hazards.

Troubleshooting

- Waterjet Cuts Poorly: nozzle wear, clogged abrasive feed, or unsecured stock.

- CNC Chatter: loose fixturing, incorrect speed/feed, or dull tool.

- Router Burns Stock: dull bit, poor feed rate, or clogged dust extraction.

- EDM Arcing or Fire: wrong dielectric, contaminated fluid, or poor grounding.

- Laser Leaves Burn Marks: dirty optics, wrong focus, or poor feed/speed settings.

- Laser Fills Shop With Smoke: inadequate ventilation or cutting improper materials.

Practical Shop Notes

- Always double-check toolpaths and setups before pressing start.

- Label coolant and dielectric tanks clearly to avoid chemical mix-ups.

- Do not bypass safety interlocks or cabinet doors.

- Never engrave unknown materials. Fumes may be toxic or corrosive.

- Keep first-aid supplies nearby. Cuts from precision machines are clean, deep, and bleed fast.

- If outsourcing, ask fabricators about safety and ventilation. Unsafe shops make unsafe parts.

That "little spark" is never just a little spark.

Section 2.14 – Miscellaneous Shop Tools & Accessories

Not every hazard in the shop comes from the big, loud machines. Many injuries happen with the smaller tools and accessories that slip under the radar. Sharpening systems, honing stones, polishing compounds, honing fluids, dust collection add-ons, magnets, and shop fixtures all seem minor compared to a forge or press. But they still carry risks of cuts, fires, or toxic exposure. This section ties together those extra tools that do not fit neatly elsewhere but are critical to shop safety.

Major Hazards

- Deep lacerations from sharpened blades.
- Fire from polishing compounds, oils, or dust.
- Toxic fumes or irritation from honing oils and chemical residues.
- Spark ignition inside vacuums or dust collectors.
- Pinched fingers from strong magnets or slipping fixtures.

PPE

- Safety glasses when sharpening, honing, or jigging.
- Cut-resistant gloves only for handling sharpened blades. Never during sharpening.
- Respirator for compounds, fluids, and dust.
- Natural-fiber aprons and clothing when working around blades.

Safe Practices

- Treat every blade on the sharpening bench as live.
- Review manufacturer instructions and safety data sheets before using compounds or fluids.
- Store stones properly. Never expose them to rapid temperature swings.
- Keep oils and compounds sealed, away from heat and sparks.
- Test jigs and fixtures carefully before applying full force.

Cords across the floor are trip hazards with extra voltage.

Troubleshooting

- Stone Cracking: improper storage or sudden temperature change. Replace.

- Uneven Edge: jig misalignment or inconsistent angle.

- Vacuum Overheating or Smelling Hot: clogged filter or possible dust ignition. Stop immediately.

- Compound Smoking: over-application or flammable compound overheated.

Practical Shop Notes

- Keep sharpening logs for consistency and to avoid overgrinding.

- Mark stones and strops by grit to avoid contamination.

- Label oils and compounds clearly.

- Empty dust collectors frequently. Fine dust is fire fuel.

- Store magnets and fixtures in racks. Not loose in drawers.

Electricity is invisible, silent, and doesn't give second chances.

Materials Handling & Disposal

Steel, wood, resin, bone, antler, synthetics, stone. These are the raw ingredients of knifemaking. Without them, there is nothing to cut, grind, shape, or forge. They are exciting to buy and rewarding to manipulate. But they also carry hazards that many makers overlook. Unlike a power tool, materials do not whir or cut. They sit quietly on shelves or pile up in bins, looking harmless. Yet they can injure, poison, or burn you if you do not respect them.

Materials have long memories. Steel rusts the moment humidity sneaks in. Exotic woods trigger allergic reactions years into a career. Dust from synthetics accumulates in your lungs whether you notice it or not. Even waste, scraps, oily rags, dust bags, lingers in the background until one day it smolders or sparks into a fire. The quiet nature of these risks makes them easy to ignore, but no less real. Proper handling is not just about protecting yourself. It is about protecting the investment you have made in your shop. A bar of tool steel is not cheap, and neither is a block of stabilized burl. Mishandling them does not only cause injury, it wastes money. Cracked handle blocks, warped G10 sheets, or rusted steel stock all represent lost opportunity. Safe, organized material management keeps you from losing dollars to mistakes before you have even turned on a grinder. On the flip side, good material handling makes you more efficient. A well-organized rack means you find the right steel quickly instead of digging through piles. Proper storage keeps dust and scraps under control so your bench is not buried before the project is half done. Waste management ensures you are not tripping over ankle-slicers disguised as future projects. The greatest dangers with materials are often invisible. A piece of scrap lying on the floor looks small. Until you step on it and drive it through your shoe. A bin of sawdust seems harmless, until a spark finds it. An oily rag smells ordinary until it self-ignites in the middle of the night. Dust is especially deceptive. From wood to composites, dust lingers in the air, sticks to surfaces, and sneaks into lungs. Over time, it does not just make the shop dirty. It damages your health permanently. Safe practices like respirators, dust collection, and smart disposal are as important as eye protection at the grinder. Material handling is not just about what is in the shop, but also about how the shop interacts with its environment. Temperature swings cause steel to sweat and rust. Humidity can cause swells and cracks in wood. Dry shops split antler and bone, while damp shops invite mold into exotic handle materials. Even stabilized materials are not immune to long-term damage when neglected. Proper storage means more than keeping things off the floor. It means thinking about climate, airflow, and long-term preservation.

Magnesium doesn't care about your water bucket, it'll just burn brighter for the show.

A small investment in humidity control or sealed bins can save hundreds in ruined materials and hours in frustration. Every cut produces waste, and every waste product needs a home. Good makers know that waste is as much a part of shop planning as tools and materials. Steel goes to scrap bins. Dust gets bagged and sealed. Handle scraps are sorted between what is usable and what belongs in the trash. Oily rags go in fire-safe cans, never in the corner of the shop. Disposal is not glamorous, but it is vital. A sloppy waste system creates clutter, hides hazards, and invites disaster. A clean one keeps the shop safe, efficient, and ready for the next project.

This section is about respect. Not just for the sharp edges and glowing forges, but for the quiet dangers that pile up underfoot and linger in the air. Respect for steel means storing it so it does not rust or roll onto your toes. Respect for wood means keeping it stable so it does not split. Respect for composites means never underestimating the harm of invisible dust. Respect for waste means taking the time to dispose of it safely, not just tossing it aside. In knifemaking, safety is not just about protecting your body. It is about protecting your materials, your tools, your shop, and your future projects. That is what this section is for: to remind you that the raw stuff of the craft and the waste it leaves behind deserves as much care as the knife itself.

That oily rag pile in the corner? Congratulations, you've built a time-delayed flamethrower.

Section 3.1 – Steel & Metals

Steel is the fundamental material in the knife shop. It is the raw material that everything else revolves around. Without steel, there are no blades to shape, no edges to sharpen, no knives to finish. But before it becomes a gleaming blade on the bench, steel is heavy, awkward, sharp-edged, and sometimes unpredictable. In many shops, it is also the first thing that can hurt you before you ever light the forge or start the grinder. Steel comes in many forms: long bars that act like battering rams when they tip over, heavy billets that strain your back if you try to lift them wrong, thin sheet stock with edges as sharp as razors, and small cut-offs that hide underfoot like caltrops waiting for a tire. And then there is the scrap pile. It is a collection of oddly shaped, oily, and sometimes still-hot pieces that attract sparks and flames like a campfire waiting to happen. For many makers, steel feels inert. It is just stock, just material, something you do not think of as dangerous until it bites you. But a careless moment while lifting, a bar stored wrong, or a bin of scrap ignored too long can lead to injuries, fires, or worse. In fact, more than a few makers have earned their first real shop scars not from the grinder, but from picking up the wrong piece of steel at the wrong time. It is also important to remember that not all steels are created equal when it comes to safety. Carbon steel dust can irritate your lungs, stainless alloys can release hazardous fumes when welded, and powdered metals can be explosive under certain conditions. Handling and storing steel properly is not just about protecting your toes or keeping the shop neat. It is about controlling fire risks, preventing toxic exposure, and making sure your materials do not become liabilities.

This section takes a closer look at the hazards of steel and metals before they become knives, focusing on storage, handling, and everyday precautions. Because while steel is the foundation of your craft, it has no problem reminding you who is really in charge if you do not respect it.

Major Hazards

- Sharp Edges: mill edges, cutoffs, and sheet metal slice skin easily.

- Weight & Bulk: strains, sprains, or crush injuries from lifting or dropping heavy stock.

- Hot Metal: recently forged or cut steel that still looks cold but is dangerously hot.

- Storage Hazards: unsecured bars rolling, falling, or tipping from racks.

- Fire Hazards: steel dust and sparks landing on oily rags or scrap piles.

- Toxicity: certain alloys (manganese, chromium, nickel, etc.) release toxic fumes when welded or ground.

You can never have too many fire extinguishers. Unless you own none, then you're already one short.

PPE

- Cut-resistant gloves when handling raw stock or scrap.

- Safety glasses for all cutting, grinding, or forging operations.

- Steel-toe boots for protection from dropped stock.

- Aprons or protective clothing to prevent cuts or burns.

- Respirator when working with stainless or alloy steels that generate hazardous dust or fumes.

Safe Practices

- Always assume freshly cut or forged steel is hot. Test with the back of your hand or tongs before grabbing.

- Store bars and billets horizontally in sturdy racks or cradles that prevent rolling. Never balance them loosely on shelves.

- For vertical storage, use a steel holder, wall-mounted rack, or floor stand with restraints or chains to secure long bars. This prevents them from tipping or sliding when bumped.

- Do not lean long stock loosely against walls. It only takes a small nudge for a bar to slip and fall.

- Organize vertical storage by length and diameter so pieces do not jam together and become unsafe to pull out.

- Use carts, dollies, or a second person to move heavy steel. Never rely on brute force alone.

- Keep scrap bins for cutoffs and grindings. Empty them regularly to avoid fire hazards.

- Deburr sharp edges before storage when possible. Especially for sheet stock.

- Mark stock with chalk or paint for alloy type and condition. It saves both safety risks and wasted effort.

- Keep oily rags, solvent containers, and other combustibles away from steel scrap piles and storage areas. Sparks can ignite soaked cloth or fine dust quickly.

- Do not overload storage racks or stands. Design them to handle the weight you are actually storing.

Your hoodie drawstring is not a safety tether. It is a lathe's favorite snack.

Practical Shop Notes

Small Shop Storage Solutions

- Wall-mounted vertical holders with chains or clamps are ideal where floor space is tight.

- PVC or metal pipe sections bolted to the wall can serve as safe vertical sleeves for bar stock.

- Rolling carts with cradles or bins let you keep steel mobile, but make sure wheels are heavy-duty and lockable.

- Avoid leaving bars standing loose in corners. They are guaranteed to tip eventually.

Large Shop Storage Solutions

- Dedicated horizontal racking systems (like pallet racks or welded steel racks) allow organized storage by alloy and size.

- Floor-mounted vertical steel holders with safety chains let you store long stock safely and access it quickly.

- Color coding or tagging racks by steel type (carbon, stainless, tool steels) prevents mix-ups and saves time.

- Use forklifts or hoists for moving billets or large sheets. Never rely on manual lifting for loads over 100 lbs.

General Best Practices

- Keep a magnet handy for quick sorting (carbon versus stainless).

- Label steel types and sizes clearly. Mystery steel is both a safety hazard and a waste of work.

- Sweep grinding areas daily to prevent fine dust from accumulating around steel storage.

- Break down scrap into manageable sizes before storing or recycling.

- Record alloy types and suppliers. Safety data and hazards can vary by steel composition

A loose workpiece does not "fall" out of the chuck. It launches.

Section 3.2 – Handle Materials(Wood, Bone, Antler, Synthetic, and Other Specialty Materials)

If steel is the skeleton of a knife, the handle is its skin. It is the part that touches the hand, carries the maker's style, and often becomes the centerpiece of the finished piece. Makers put enormous effort into choosing handle materials that stand out: exotic hardwoods with wild figure, rich antler or bone with organic texture, sleek modern synthetics like G10, or even rare and prized materials like fossilized mammoth ivory. But, beauty does not come without cost. These materials, while stunning, bring unique hazards into the shop that are easy to overlook. Many exotic hardwoods contain natural chemicals that can cause allergic reactions, skin rashes, or long-term respiratory problems. Bone and antler grind into pungent dust that can carry microbes if not properly treated. Synthetics like G10 and carbon fiber produce dust that is not only irritating to the skin but also damaging to the lungs if inhaled. Resins used in stabilization or casting can cause burns, eye damage, or chemical sensitivity if handled without care. Even stone or fossil materials, which may look solid and harmless, create fine silica dust when cut or polished. This is a substance linked to serious lung disease.

Handle work adds artistry to the craft, but it can also add hidden dangers. This section provides a clear look at the risks tied to wood, bone, antler, synthetics, and other specialty handle materials, along with the protective measures that keep makers safe while still allowing creativity to flourish.

Major Hazards

Wood

- Toxic dust from exotic and some common woods (for example, cocobolo, rosewood, oak, walnut).
- Allergic reactions, dermatitis, and long-term respiratory illness.
- Highly flammable fine dust.

Bone & Antler

- Dust inhalation with unpleasant odor and harmful particulates.
- Risk of microbial contamination in raw material.
- Splintering under saws or grinders.

Lathe chips are not curls. They are nature's barbed wire.

Synthetics (G10, Carbon Fiber, Micarta)

- Extremely fine fiberglass or carbon dust embeds in lungs and skin.

- Resin irritation to eyes and skin.

- Accumulated dust is flammable.

Ivory & Mammoth Tooth/Bone

- Dust can carry similar risks to bone and stone. This includes microbial or silica exposure.

- Cracking during grinding may send sharp fragments airborne.

- Legal and ethical issues with ivory must also be considered.

Stone (Jade, Agate, Fossilized Materials)

- Cutting and polishing produces silica dust, which can cause silicosis.

- Breakage under cutting tools may create flying shards.

- Requires water cooling. Dry grinding is extremely hazardous.

Resins & Stabilization

- Liquid resins (epoxy, polyester, urethane) can cause severe skin or eye irritation.

- Fumes during curing can be toxic in enclosed spaces.

- Hardened resins create fine dust that is irritating and flammable.

PPE

- Respirator (P100 filters). Non-negotiable when sanding wood, bone, antler, stone, or synthetics.

- Eye Protection: glasses or sealed goggles when cutting or grinding brittle materials like bone, stone, or fossil.

- Gloves: nitrile gloves for resin handling; cut-resistant gloves for sharp offcuts.

- Clothing: long sleeves when sanding synthetics or stone to prevent fiberglass or silica irritation.

- Ventilation: dust collection, fume extraction, or outdoor work for resins and stabilizers.

Wood blanks do not "split." They explode at face-shield velocity.

Safe Practices

- Always check a wood toxicity chart before cutting or sanding unfamiliar woods.

- Handle bone, antler, and ivory only when thoroughly dried and cleaned to reduce microbial hazards.

- Grind stone and fossil materials wet to keep dust down. Never dry cut.

- Stabilize soft woods, bone, or antler before heavy shaping to reduce splintering and dust.

- When mixing or casting resins, wear gloves and goggles, and work in well-ventilated areas. Never cure resins in an enclosed shop without ventilation.

- Keep sanding belts and grinding wheels dedicated to specific materials when possible to avoid cross-contamination of steel and synthetics.

- Never burn offcuts of G10, carbon fiber, or resin. Fumes are toxic. Bag and dispose of them as waste.

- Wash hands, arms, and face after working with dust or resins. Do not carry it into your home or onto your family.

Practical Shop Notes

- Keep a toxicity chart posted in the shop for wood species and common handle materials.

- Label all blocks, scales, and handle materials clearly so you know what you are working with.

- Use a dedicated small shop vac or extractor for handle materials only. Do not share with steel grinding sparks.

- Store bone, antler, and ivory in sealed containers to prevent odor, contamination, and cracking.

- Wet-grind stone and fossil materials with plenty of water flow and a drainage plan. It reduces both dust and tool wear.

- Keep a separate disposal bag for synthetic dust and resin scraps. Never sweep them into the general shop trash.

Gloves near a lathe? That is just finger origami practice.

Section 3.3 – Hazardous Materials (Epoxy, Resins, Adhesives)

Knifemaking does not stop at steel and handles. It is held together, sealed, and finished with chemistry. Epoxies, resins, and adhesives are indispensable in the shop, but they are also among the more hazardous materials you will work with. Unlike cuts or burns, chemical exposures do not always hurt right away. The danger often shows up later, in the form of rashes, breathing problems, eye damage, or long-term sensitivity that makes you unable to use certain products at all. The challenge with chemicals is their deceptive nature. You can see a grinder spark or feel a hot piece of steel, but most chemical risks are invisible. Fumes in the air, microscopic dust from sanding cured epoxy, or a thin layer of adhesive that lingers on your skin after wiping away excess can cause problems. Even when the smell fades, the hazard often remains. Makers often assume that if something does not feel dangerous in the moment, it must be safe. Unfortunately, that assumption has left many with lifelong chemical sensitivities or chronic reactions. Another issue is routine. It is easy to become careless with materials you use every day. Mixing epoxy without gloves just this once, pouring resin in a closed room because it is cold outside, or sanding an old glue joint without a respirator. Over time, these little shortcuts add up. The body can only take so much exposure before it begins to react, sometimes suddenly and severely. A maker who develops epoxy sensitivity, for example, may find themselves unable to even walk into a shop where it is being mixed without breaking into rashes or struggling to breathe. Finally, there is the problem of waste and storage. Many adhesives and resins remain chemically active until fully cured, meaning they can continue releasing fumes or even start fires if not disposed of correctly. Storing them improperly, such as leaving containers in direct sunlight, near heat sources, or without proper sealing, can cause leaks, dangerous fumes, or even explosions.

This section covers the safe handling, storage, and disposal of epoxies, resins, and adhesives commonly used in knife shops. By respecting the risks and using the right protective measures, you can keep bonding your workpieces together without accidentally bonding yourself to a lifetime of chemical problems.

Major Hazards

Epoxies

- Skin irritation, chemical burns, and long-term sensitization.

- Dust from sanding cured epoxy can cause respiratory irritation.

- Improperly mixed epoxy may remain uncured and hazardous.

Unclamped blades do not wait politely. They spin like angry propellers.

Resins (Polyester, Polyurethane, Casting Resins)

- Release volatile organic compounds (VOCs) and toxic fumes during mixing and curing.

- Can cause headaches, nausea, and long-term respiratory illness with poor ventilation.

- Highly flammable when in liquid state.

Adhesives (CA Glue, Contact Cement, Industrial Glues)

- Eye and respiratory irritation from fumes.

- Bonding skin instantly (superglue accidents are common).

- Flammability risks in enclosed spaces.

PPE

- Respirator with organic vapor cartridges for mixing and curing resins or using adhesives with fumes.

- Nitrile gloves (not latex — many chemicals eat through latex quickly).

- Eye protection. Splashes can cause serious eye damage.

- Protective clothing. Old shirts or aprons to protect against spills.

Safe Practices

- Mix resins and epoxies in well-ventilated areas or under a fume hood. Never in a sealed room.

- Follow manufacturer mix ratios exactly. Improper mixes may stay sticky and hazardous.

- Avoid skin contact. Even small repeated exposures can cause sensitization (permanent allergic reactions).

- Label all containers clearly, especially secondary containers.

- Never eat or drink near adhesives, resins, or epoxies.

- Sand cured resin or epoxy only with dust collection and a respirator.

- Dispose of resin and adhesive waste properly. Never pour liquids down drains. Allow leftover resin or epoxy to cure fully before disposal.

- Store adhesives in sealed containers away from heat sources.

Hot steel doesn't care if you're experienced. Neither does gravity.

Practical Shop Notes

- Keep a dedicated chemicals corner with proper ventilation and spill protection.

- Store resins and adhesives in sealed, upright containers away from direct sunlight or heat.

- Write the date opened on containers. Many resins and adhesives degrade over time.

- Keep Material Safety Data Sheets (MSDS) for every product in your shop. They are often available online from the manufacturer.

- If a spill occurs, absorb with vermiculite, cat litter, or shop absorbent, then bag and dispose of according to local regulations.

- Keep acetone or debonder on hand for accidental CA glue skin bonding. Never pull skin apart by force.

Disposal Considerations

- Cure before disposal. If you have leftover resin or epoxy, mix in the correct ratio and let it cure fully in a disposable container. Hardened blocks can usually go in the trash.

- Absorb liquids. For small spills or leftover adhesives, mix with vermiculite, cat litter, or shop absorbent until solidified. Bag and label before disposal.

- Segregate waste. Do not mix chemical waste with steel or wood scraps. Use a small labeled hazard bin for resins, epoxies, and adhesives.

- Local regulations: Household Hazardous Waste programs (HHW) in many cities and counties will accept small quantities. Small shops may qualify under household rules if quantities are low. Larger operations may be subject to EPA Small Quantity Generator rules.

- Transport rules: Facilities may require chemicals in original containers or clearly labeled sealed containers.

- Storage before disposal: Keep containers sealed, upright, and away from heat or sunlight while waiting for proper disposal.

- Never burn or dump. Burning adhesives, epoxies, or resins produces highly toxic fumes. Dumping risks groundwater contamination.

Hazardous Materials

Your hammer never misses the steel as often as it misses your finger… until one day it decides to make up for lost time.

Section 3.4 – Toxic Dusts
(G10, Carbon Fiber, Exotic Woods)

In most shops, dust is treated like background noise. It is the stuff you sweep up at the end of the day or brush off your shirt before heading inside. Compared to the crazy tools, machines, and motors, dust feels harmless. It is just a mess, not a threat. And that is exactly why it is so dangerous. The reality is that dust is one of the most silent and persistent hazards in a knife shop. Unlike sparks, it does not demand your attention. Unlike sharp steel, it does not cut you instantly. Dust hangs in the air invisibly, drifts into your lungs, coats your skin, and lingers long after the machines are shut down. By the time you notice the damage, it is too late to undo. Not all dust is created equal. Woodworkers have long known that some species of wood, like cocobolo, rosewood, or walnut, can cause allergic reactions, skin irritation, or asthma-like symptoms. Knife makers push those risks further, introducing modern composites like G10 and carbon fiber. These materials are engineered for strength, but that strength comes from glass-like fibers and resins that, once airborne, act like millions of microscopic needles. They do not break down in the lungs. They do not dissolve. They stay, lodged in tissue, where the body struggles and fails to get rid of them. Even so-called safe dust, from oak, maple, or general grinding, are not harmless. In high enough quantities, any fine dust can scar lung tissue, inflame airways, and build up into long-term health problems. Add in stone, fossil, or ivory dust, which can mimic silica exposure, and the risks multiply. What makes dust uniquely hazardous is that it does not hurt right away. You will not feel a burn like you would from hot steel. You will not hear a snap like when a belt breaks. Instead, the damage creeps in over years: a cough that lingers, skin that reacts more often, a shortness of breath you cannot quite explain. Many makers have shrugged off that first cough or itch only to find, years later, that they cannot work with certain materials at all without risking their health. The good news is that dust hazards are manageable with the right practices. Respirators, dust collection systems, smart work habits, and proper disposal can all keep the risks under control. But they only work if they are used consistently. Skipping a mask just this once, or sanding in an unventilated space because it is convenient, is how long-term damage starts.

This section looks past the surface and dives into dust as a serious safety issue in the knife shop. It explains how dust harms the body, why certain materials are worse than others, and how to set up shop practices that protect your health for the long haul. Dust may not shout like a grinder or glow like a forge, but it can be just as deadly if ignored.

Gas vapor does not flare. It explodes enthusiastically.

Physical Damages from Dust Exposure

Lungs & Respiratory System

- Ultrafine dust particles bypass the body's natural defenses (nose hairs, mucus) and embed in lung tissue.
- Long-term exposure to carbon fiber, G10, or exotic wood dust can cause chronic bronchitis, asthma-like symptoms, or even pulmonary fibrosis (lung scarring).
- Some exotic wood species are linked to sensitization. Once you are allergic, you may react violently even to tiny exposures.

Eyes

- Fine fiberglass or wood dust causes irritation, redness, and in some cases scratches to the cornea.
- Eye exposure is often overlooked but can lead to recurring inflammation.

Skin

- Fiberglass-like particles from G10 and carbon fiber cause rashes and itching (similar to insulation rash).
- Oils and resins in exotic woods can trigger contact dermatitis (itchy or blistered skin).

Long-Term Risks

- Fine dust exposure over years can lead to decreased lung function and chronic health conditions.
- Silica-like dust from fossil materials or stone handles has been linked to silicosis, a severe, incurable lung disease.

PPE – Your First Line of Defense

- Respirators: Always use a properly fitted respirator with P100 filters when working with G10, carbon fiber, or exotic woods. Paper dust masks are inadequate.
- Eye Protection: Use sealed goggles if dust is heavy, especially with fiberglass materials.
- Skin Protection: Wear long sleeves and gloves when working with synthetics to prevent fiberglass rash.
- Dedicated Clothing: Keep dusty clothing out of your home laundry. Use a shop-only work shirt or apron.

Superglue has saved more shop sessions than we admit, but remember, it is meant to hold the skin closed, not keep your pride intact.

Safe Practices for Working with Toxic Dusts

- Dust Collection: Use localized dust extraction (grinder hoods, sanding table vacuums) with HEPA filters.

- Wet Methods: When possible, wet-grind stone, fossil, or silica-based materials to prevent airborne dust.

- Respirable crystalline silica from stone and fossil materials is regulated by OSHA 1910.1053. Wet methods and P100 respirators keep exposure well below the permissible limit.

- Do not use Compressed Air: Never blow dust off with air. It launches particles into the air where they stay for hours. Use the appropriate vacuum.

- Separate Work Areas: If possible, separate your dusty work area (wood and synthetics) from steel grinding to reduce fire risks.

- Housekeeping: Sweep and vacuum with HEPA filters regularly. Regular shop vacs without filters just recirculate fine dust.

- Personal Hygiene: Wash hands, arms, and face immediately after dusty work. Shower if you have been working with fiberglass-like materials.

Disposal of Dust and Waste

- Bag and Seal: Collect dust in sealed bags (contractor-grade trash bags work well). Do not sweep dust directly into shop trash cans where it can escape.

- Segregate: Keep dust from synthetics (G10, carbon fiber) separate from wood dust. Never burn or compost synthetic dust.

- Never Burn: Burning G10, carbon fiber, or resin-based dust releases highly toxic fumes. Wood dust can be burned, but only if it is clean and local regulations allow.

- Vacuum Maintenance: Empty dust collectors frequently to reduce fire hazards. Fine dust piles plus grinder sparks equals shop fire.

- Check Local Rules: Many municipalities treat synthetic dust and resin waste like chemical waste. Bagged wood dust usually can go to landfill.

The phrase "I have got it" is apprentice speak for I am about to do something dumb.

Practical Shop Notes

- Keep a toxicity reference chart posted in the shop for wood species and composites.

- Dedicate one shop vac to wood and synthetic dust and another to steel dust. Never mix them.

- Upgrade filters to HEPA grade for dust collection.

- Wear your respirator when cleaning the shop. Sweeping and vacuuming release as much dust as grinding.

- Store bagged dust in sealed bins until disposal day.

Kids can find the sharpest tool in the shop faster than you can say "stay out."

Section 3.5 – Chemicals, Solvents & Oils

Chemicals, Solvents & Oils

A knife shop often feels defined by its noise and heat. But in the quiet corners of the shop, stacked on shelves or tucked under benches, lie bottles and cans of chemicals that are just as dangerous as any machine. They do not spark, they do not roar, and they do not glow red hot. But they can poison, burn, blind, or set your shop ablaze if handled carelessly. The most dangerous thing about chemicals in a shop is how ordinary they appear. A quart of acetone looks like water. A jug of mineral spirits smells like cleaning fluid. A bottle of quench oil could be mistaken for motor oil. These materials do not scream hazard, but the risks they carry are serious. Solvents like acetone or denatured alcohol can fill a room with invisible vapors in minutes, leaving you lightheaded and sick. Or worse, one spark away from an explosion. Oils that seem harmless can cause flash fires or spontaneous combustion if left on rags. Even simple household products like bleach or WD-40 become hazardous when mixed with the wrong chemical or exposed to heat. Then there are the specialty shop chemicals: ferric chloride for etching, acids for cleaning, stabilizers for handle materials, polishes and waxes for finishing. Each has its place in a maker's workflow, and each brings a hidden hazard: corrosive burns, toxic fumes, or flammable vapors. A splash of acid, a tipped container of quench oil, or even a forgotten rag can turn a productive day into a dangerous one. The real problem is complacency. Because these chemicals are so familiar, it is easy to treat them casually. A rag left to dry on the bench. A solvent used indoors without ventilation because it is cold outside. A quench tank heated just a little too much. Over time, these small lapses add up. And one day, they become the cause of a fire, an injury, or a serious health issue.

This section takes a thorough look at the wide range of chemicals, solvents, and oils commonly found in knife shops: from the everyday standbys like WD-40 and 3-in-1 oil, to specialized acids and stabilizers. It explains their hazards, outlines the protective equipment you need, and provides clear safe practices for storage, handling, and disposal. Because while chemicals may sit quietly on a shelf, they demand the same respect you would give to a running grinder or a glowing forge.

Major Hazards by Category

Solvents (Acetone, Alcohols, Mineral Spirits, Paint Thinner)

- Highly flammable vapors, invisible and fast-spreading.

- Eye and lung irritation; long-term exposure can damage the nervous system.

- Rapid evaporation can leave explosive concentrations in unventilated spaces.

A visitor's favorite phrase is "I've got it."

Cutting Oils & Quench Oils

- Fire hazards when exposed to sparks or overheated steel.
- Burns from splashes during quenching.
- Oil-soaked rags are a leading cause of spontaneous combustion fires.
- Slippery floors and fall hazards from spills.

Light & Household Oils (3-in-1, Penetrating Oils, WD-40)

- Flammable vapors; risk if used near open flame or grinders.
- Skin irritation with repeated exposure.
- Some create toxic gases if exposed to welding heat (for example, chlorinated cleaners).

Cleaning Supplies (Bleach, Degreasers, Detergents)

- Chemical burns or skin irritation on contact.
- Mixing bleach with acids or ammonia creates poisonous gases.
- Many degreasers are flammable.

Acids (Ferric Chloride, Hydrochloric, Vinegar Solutions for Etching)

- Severe skin and eye burns.
- Corrosive to shop surfaces and containers if not handled properly.
- Dangerous fumes must always be used with ventilation.

Stabilizing Resins & Hardeners

- Skin and eye irritants.
- Release volatile organic compounds (VOCs).
- Flammable before curing.

Waxes, Polishes, and Finishing Compounds

- May contain solvents or petroleum distillates.
- Flammable when applied near hot equipment.
- Some create fine dusts that are both inhalation hazards and combustible.

Shop tour is Latin for "find the sharpest thing and touch it."

PPE

- Gloves: nitrile gloves for most solvents, oils, and acids. Avoid latex.

- Eye Protection: safety glasses with side shields or goggles, especially with acids and solvents.

- Respirator: organic vapor cartridges for solvents, degreasers, or acid fumes.

- Protective Clothing: shop coats or aprons that resist chemical soaking.

Safe Practices

- Work with solvents and acids only in well-ventilated areas or outdoors.

- Keep flammable liquids in approved safety cans or sealed original containers.

- Store chemicals in a dedicated cabinet. Ideally a flammable storage cabinet.

- Separate acids from solvents and oils; never store them together.

- Clean up spills immediately using absorbent (vermiculite, cat litter, shop absorbent).

- Never store chemicals in food containers or unlabeled bottles.

- Dispose of oily rags in a metal container with a self-closing lid to prevent spontaneous combustion.

- Warm quench oils slowly and never leave unattended. Keep a metal lid nearby to smother flare-ups.

- When mixing acids (like ferric chloride), always add acid to water, never the reverse.

- Never weld, grind, or cut near solvent vapors. Invisible fumes can ignite.

- Keep an eyewash station or portable eyewash bottle readily available when working with acids or solvents.

Practical Shop Notes

- Buy chemicals in smaller containers. Easier to store, less risk if spilled.

- Keep Safety Data Sheets (SDS) for every chemical and material in an easily accessible binder or digital folder.

- Rotate stock; old oils and solvents degrade and may form sludge or dangerous compounds.

- Label every container. Future you will not remember what jar A was.

- Keep a spill kit with vermiculite, absorbent pads, gloves, and disposal bags within arm's reach.

- For acids, use plastic trays or tubs to contain drips and prevent corrosion of benches.

- Keep chemical fire extinguishers (Class B) near storage areas.

The shop doesn't care that you're having a bad day. It's still going to try to kill you.

Disposal Considerations

Solvents (Acetone, Alcohols, Mineral Spirits)

- Never pour down drains. Treat as hazardous waste.
- Store in sealed containers until they can be taken to Household Hazardous Waste (HHW) facilities.
- Some automotive shops accept small solvent quantities.

Oils (Quench Oils, Cutting Oils, 3-in-1, Penetrating Oils)

- Collect used oils in a metal container with a tight lid.
- Do not dump in trash or drains; most auto shops and recycling centers accept used oils.
- Dispose of oil-soaked rags in metal rag cans with self-closing lids to prevent spontaneous combustion.

Acids (Ferric Chloride, Hydrochloric, Vinegar, etc.)

- Store in labeled plastic containers until HHW disposal.
- Neutralize small batches of mild acids (vinegar, citric solutions) with baking soda before disposal if permitted locally.
- Never mix acids with other waste streams.

Cleaning Supplies

- Keep in original containers until disposal.
- Do not combine leftovers. Many HHW programs accept bleach and cleaners.

Waxes & Polishes

- Allow used rags to dry outdoors before disposal.
- Solidified wax or polish can usually be discarded with household trash once hardened.

A clean shop is a happy shop. A messy one is a very expensive lesson.

Section 3.6 – Material Storage & Organization

A knife maker's shop is often judged by its layout, its tools, or the knives coming off the bench. But look closer, and you will see the real foundation in the way materials are stored. Steel bars tucked in corners, handle blocks piled in boxes, or a sheet of G10 leaning against a wall may not look dangerous, but the truth is that how you store your materials determines both your efficiency and your safety. Improperly stored steel can be like a spring trap. One wrong move and a stack of bars can tumble, crushing feet or damaging tools. Handle materials are just as risky in their own way. A block of exotic wood that absorbs moisture may crack, warp, or even grow mold. Bone, antler, or ivory left in fluctuating humidity can split or delaminate. Synthetics like G10 or Micarta resist many hazards, but they too can warp if stored leaning against a wall or degrade when exposed to constant heat and sunlight. The challenges do not stop at accidents and damage. Poor organization can cost you valuable time. Hunting for that one piece of stabilized maple you swear you bought, or realizing halfway through a project that your mystery steel might not be the alloy you thought it was.

Unlabeled materials become wasted money, wasted effort, and sometimes unsafe substitutions that compromise a blade's integrity. Temperature and humidity play bigger roles than many makers realize. Steel sweats with condensation when shop temperatures swing, quickly leading to rust if left untreated. Wood will expand and contract with moisture, sometimes warping beyond use. Bone and ivory are notoriously temperamental. They are stable in controlled conditions but prone to cracking if the shop is too dry. Even stabilized woods, which resist these changes better than natural stock, can suffer if stored for months in a damp basement or a sunlit window.

A well-organized and climate-aware material storage system not only keeps your shop safer but also protects your investments. Quality steels and exotic handle materials are not cheap, and losing them to rust, cracks, or accidents is money you will never get back. More importantly, proper storage helps prevent injuries. Because in a cluttered shop, it is not the knife that gets you first, it is often the pile of steel you trip over on the way to the grinder.

This section explores the practical and safe ways to store, label, and organize all the materials common to knifemaking: steel stock, handle blocks, synthetics, and fragile specialty items. It also takes a closer look at how environmental factors like temperature and humidity affect those materials, so you can make small changes that keep your shop safe, efficient, and ready for the next project.

> Organization isn't about looking neat. It's about not dying in a stupid way.

Major Hazards

Steel Stock (bars, rods, sheet)

- Heavy pieces can fall, crush toes, or injure hands.

- Long stock leaning against walls can tip or slide unexpectedly.

- Rust and burrs may cut unprotected hands.

Handle Materials (woods, bones, antlers, stones, fossils)

- Splinters, chips, and sharp edges.

- Dust or mold buildup in poorly ventilated storage.

- Breakage of brittle or stabilized pieces.

- Warping or cracking in unstable temperature or humidity.

Synthetic Materials (G10, Micarta, Carbon Fiber)

- Warp or crack if not stored flat.

- UV light can degrade resins over time.

- Edges chip easily if dropped.

General Storage Risks

- Tripping hazards from clutter.

- Fire hazards if flammable handle materials are kept near sparks or solvents.

- Losing track of material inventory leads to wasted money and unsafe substitutions.

Environmental Considerations

Temperature

- Extreme heat can soften epoxies in stabilized woods and weaken resin-based synthetics.

- Cold alone rarely damages materials, but cycles of heating and cooling cause wood to expand and contract, leading to cracks.

- Steel should be stored in a consistent, moderate-temperature area to avoid condensation.

That random pile of scrap on the bench? It's plotting against you.

Humidity

- Wood is the most vulnerable. High humidity causes swelling and mold; low humidity causes drying and cracking. Aim for 40–60 percent relative humidity.

- Bone, antler, and ivory are also sensitive to drying. They shrink, split, or delaminate if humidity fluctuates.

- Steel rusts rapidly in damp air; use oil coatings, silica packs, or dehumidifiers in storage spaces.

- Synthetics (G10, Micarta) resist humidity, but they still absorb some moisture over time if left unsealed.

PPE When Handling Materials

- Gloves: cut-resistant gloves when moving large steel stock; nitrile gloves when handling dusty or treated handle materials.

- Eye Protection: when cutting bands, straps, or packaging around steel bundles.

- Footwear: closed-toe, preferably steel-toe boots, especially when moving heavy steel bars.

Safe Practices

- Store long steel vertically in dedicated steel racks or tubes anchored to the wall. Never lean stock loosely against a corner.

- Use horizontal racks or shelving for shorter bars and offcuts. Label by type (1095, 5160, stainless, Damascus, etc.).

- Coat stored steels lightly with oil or rust-preventative spray, especially in humid climates.

- Keep handle materials sorted and labeled by type and treatment (stabilized, natural, exotics).

- Store synthetics flat to prevent warping; cover from direct sunlight to avoid UV damage.

- Separate flammable handle materials (wood, bone dust, Micarta offcuts) from welding, grinding, or chemical storage.

- Keep fragile items like stones, ivory, and fossils in padded bins or wrapped in paper to prevent chipping.

- Maintain a first-in, first-out system. Use older materials first to avoid degradation or waste.

- Use climate control (dehumidifiers, sealed bins with silica packs, humidifiers for dry climates) to keep conditions stable.

- Keep aisles and floor space clear of stored stock to reduce tripping hazards.

Good lighting prevents accidents. Bad lighting creates YouTube videos titled "Darwin Award Nominee."

Practical Shop Notes

- Use PVC tubes or vertical racks for organizing long round bars or square stock.

- Pallet racking or wall-mounted shelves keep steel organized and off the floor.

- Plastic bins with lids are ideal for small handle blocks, preventing dust and moisture.

- Label all materials clearly. Include species for woods, grade or alloy for steels, and whether materials are stabilized.

- Keep a digital or notebook inventory so you do not double-buy materials you already have.

- For small shops with limited space, wall racks and under-bench drawers maximize efficiency while reducing clutter.

- Even in the smallest shops, a simple dehumidifier or silica packs can prevent rust and cracking without expensive HVAC.

Your shop isn't haunted. It's just waiting for you to get complacent.

Section 3.7 – Scrap & Waste Management

No matter how carefully you plan, every project produces leftovers. The short end of a steel bar, the handle block that cracked halfway through shaping, the pile of dust and shavings that gathers under the grinder. These scraps are inevitable. At first, they do not look like much. A small pile here, a bucket of offcuts there. But over time, scraps grow into one of the most common and underestimated hazards in a knife shop. Every maker has told themselves, I will save that piece for later. And sometimes it is true. A sliver of Micarta becomes a spacer, a small block of hardwood gets used for pins, or a short bit of steel finds life as a test coupon. But more often, those scraps collect under benches, get shoved into corners, or overflow bins until they turn into a mountain of tripping hazards, sharp edges, and fire risks. The dream of future projects quietly transforms into ankle-shredders, flat-tire makers, and dust bombs. The hazards are real. A steel shard in the wrong place can puncture your shoe or embed in a tire. A dust-filled vacuum, left unchecked, is one stray spark away from igniting like a firework. Oily rags tossed in the wrong bin can smolder overnight, leading to a fire that does not care how many hours of work are sitting on your bench. And handle scraps, especially synthetics, not only clutter space but can release toxic fumes if burned or handled carelessly. Scrap and waste management is not glamorous, and it rarely feels urgent at the moment. But it is one of the simplest ways to keep your shop safer, cleaner, and more efficient. By treating scrap like any other material, something that needs a home, a plan, and a safe disposal route, you protect yourself, your tools, and your projects. And as a bonus, a well-managed scrap system saves you money. You will find the useful pieces faster, stop tripping over the junk, and keep the hazards out of your path.

In short, scraps are a fact of life in a knife shop. But whether they are harmless leftovers or hidden hazards depends entirely on how you handle them. This section looks at the dangers of scrap and waste, and lays out practical, realistic systems for managing them without turning your shop into a landfill or your trash can into a bonfire.

Major Hazards

Metal Scrap & Offcuts

- Sharp edges can cut skin.
- Small pieces on the floor create puncture or tripping hazards.
- Larger offcuts stacked unsafely may fall.

Handle Material Waste

- Dust from sawing and sanding creates inhalation hazards.
- Flammable scraps (wood, Micarta, G10) stored near sparks or heat can ignite.
- Small pieces can splinter if stepped on.
- Warping or cracking in unstable temperature or humidity.

A place for everything and everything in its place… or you're about to lose a finger.

Dust & Sweepings

- Dust buildup in vacuums or collection bins create a major fire hazard when combined with sparks.
- Toxic dust (G10, exotic woods, carbon fiber) requires careful disposal.

Oily Rags & Absorbents

- High risk of spontaneous combustion if left in open trash cans.
- Fire risk even days after being soaked.

PPE

- Gloves: cut-resistant gloves when handling metal scraps.
- Eye Protection: goggles when emptying vacuums or dust bins.
- Respirator: P100 mask when dealing with fine dust waste.
- Footwear: closed-toe shoes to protect from sharp scrap underfoot.

Safe Practices

- Collect metal scraps in dedicated bins. Sharp edges down, heavy items at the bottom.
- Sweep the floor regularly. Do not let small offcuts accumulate where they can puncture shoes or tires.
- Segregate flammable handle scraps (wood, synthetics) from hot-work areas.
- Empty dust collection bins frequently. Do not wait until they are full.
- Use metal containers with lids for oily rags or absorbents. Never toss them into general trash.
- Keep a schedule for trash removal to avoid buildup.
- Store bins away from grinders, welders, and forges to reduce fire risk.
- Clearly label bins for different waste types (scrap steel, non-ferrous metals, flammable handle scraps, general trash).

Disposal Considerations

Metal Scraps

- Recycle steel and non-ferrous metals (brass, copper, bronze) where possible.
- Small unusable pieces should still go to scrap metal bins, not general trash.

Clutter doesn't just slow you down, it waits for the perfect moment to strike.

Handle Scraps

- Wood scraps can be burned in outdoor firepits if safe and legal locally.
- Synthetic scraps (G10, Micarta, carbon fiber) must go to landfill in sealed bags. Never burn. Fumes are toxic.

Dust Waste

- Always bag dust tightly before disposal.
- Keep synthetic dust separate from wood dust.
- Check local rules for hazardous waste handling of composites.

Oily Rags

- Dispose of through local hazardous waste programs if available.
- If storing temporarily, keep them in a self-closing metal can until collection.

Practical Shop Notes

- Invest in stackable scrap bins with labels for easier sorting.
- Keep one small container near the workbench and empty it daily into larger bins.
- Save handle offcuts only if they are large enough for liners, spacers, or small projects. Otherwise, let them go.
- Keep a magnet on hand for sweeping up steel chips.
- For small shops, rolling bins make it easier to clear floor space quickly.

If you have to move three things to reach one tool, you're doing it wrong.

Woodworking & Handle Making

Handles are where knives meet people. A blade may do the cutting, but it is the handle that determines how safely and comfortably that cut happens. Whether the construction is simple scales, a hidden tang, or something more ornate, this part of knife making is more deceptively hazardous. The dangers are quieter than sparks from grinding or the beat of a hammer. This makes them easier to overlook, but no less real. Handle work often produces more injuries than forging. This is not because it is more dangerous in an obvious way. It is because it is where complacency creeps in. A splinter, a nick from a carving knife, or a minor burn from a finishing rag are still injuries. Just because they are not dramatic does not make them acceptable. Every cut, irritation, and mishap adds up. Left unchecked, these little problems can slow work, compromise craftsmanship, and in some cases lead to long-term harm. Unlike forging or grinding, handle making requires a different rhythm. It is slower, more detailed, and more artistic. But the risks shift with that change of pace. Dust from exotic woods and resins does not burn like an ember, but it lingers in your lungs. Adhesives seem harmless until they sensitize your skin permanently. Power tools designed for boards and beams become unpredictable when applied to a small, irregular block of wood. Even the simple act of applying oil for a finish carries fire hazards when rags are left unattended. Patience is the safeguard here. Handle making rewards steady, careful progress and punishes haste. Impatience leads to gaps around pins, uneven finishes, ruined handles, and injuries that often come when attention wavers. Several important themes carry forward through handle making. Dust and fumes are invisible hazards from sanding, burning, and adhesives and they are some of the most dangerous. The size of the tool versus the size of the workpiece increases the chance of catches, slips, and ejections when you work with small pieces. Chemicals and flash hazards from adhesives, oils, and finishes all carry risks that extend well beyond the bench. Creativity with discipline is essential. Specialty techniques like inlays, carving, or turning showcase artistry, but they must always be balanced with caution.

Handle making is where knife building becomes personal. It is where the maker's hand, eye, and style leave their mark. But artistry and safety must go hand in hand. Every step, from choosing wood to sealing the final finish, demands awareness, patience, and respect for the hazards. When done with discipline, handle making produces not only a beautiful and functional grip but also a safe, sustainable practice for the maker.

If it smells like melting plastic, it's not "working hard", it's about to work you over.

Section 4.1 – Wood Selection & Toxicity

Wood has been the material of choice for knife handles for centuries. It is timeless, versatile, and beautiful. From the plain strength of oak to the shimmering figure of stabilized maple burl, wood has an appeal that synthetics cannot match. It feels alive, warm in the hand, and uniquely individual from piece to piece. But wood has another side. One that is not often talked about until it is too late. Most makers begin by thinking of wood as harmless. After all, you grew up around it. Furniture, flooring, firewood. It is just wood, right? But in the shop, where saws, grinders, and sanders turn it into fine dust, even the friendliest piece of maple or walnut becomes something very different. That dust fills the air, clings to your clothes, and works its way deep into your lungs. You might not feel it after a day or two, but repeated exposure adds up. And while one person may shrug it off, another may find themselves sneezing, wheezing, or breaking out in rashes. The danger is that wood toxicity often creeps up slowly. Many makers report working exotic woods like cocobolo or rosewood for years before developing allergies. Then, seemingly overnight, their body decides enough. Eyes water. Skin itches. Breathing gets tight. That once-favorite handle material becomes off-limits forever. Asthma triggered by wood dust is especially serious. Once you are sensitized, each exposure tends to make the reaction worse. For some, just walking into a dusty shop after years of exposure can cause a flare-up. And it is not only the exotics that cause trouble. Domestic hardwoods like walnut, oak, or maple have all been linked to respiratory irritation and allergic reactions. Even softwoods, with their resins and oils, can bother sensitive individuals. Stabilized woods, often thought of as safe, still carry risks. The resins used in stabilization create fine particulate dust when cut or sanded, and that dust is no better for your lungs than any other synthetic material. Wood also carries physical risks: splinters from rough stock, sharp chips when a brittle block breaks, or cracks that ruin hours of work. But the bigger, quieter dangers are the ones that sneak in with every breath you take.

This is why choosing, handling, and disposing of wood properly is critical in a knife shop. It is not about avoiding wood. It is about respecting it. With the right PPE, safe practices, and awareness of your own body's responses, wood remains one of the most rewarding handle materials you can work with. Ignore those precautions, and it becomes one of the most dangerous.

Major Hazards

Toxicity

- Exotics like cocobolo, rosewood, and ebony contain natural oils that cause skin irritation or respiratory issues.

- Domestic hardwoods like walnut or oak can still trigger allergic responses in sensitive individuals.

- Long-term exposure may lead to asthma, dermatitis, or sensitization (developing allergies over time).

> Fatigue doesn't make you look tough. It makes you look like a future statistic.

Allergies & Asthma

- Many makers develop sensitivity after years of exposure. A wood that was harmless at first can eventually cause rashes, watery eyes, or wheezing.

- Asthma triggered by wood dust is a serious risk, especially with exotics. Once sensitized, reactions can become stronger with every exposure.

- Stabilized woods contain dust and resin particles that can trigger reactions.

Dust Hazards

- Fine sanding dust penetrates deep into lungs and often causes more harm than larger particles.

- Stabilized woods contain resin that, when cut or sanded, produces synthetic dust harmful to breathe.

Physical Hazards

- Splinters and chips from rough handling.

- Cracks or unstable wood that fails during shaping.

PPE

- Respirator: a P100 or organic vapor cartridge respirator for sanding and shaping wood, especially exotics or stabilized woods.

- Eye Protection: safety glasses or goggles. Dust and chips travel farther than you think.

- Gloves: nitrile or work gloves when handling raw exotics to prevent skin contact reactions.

- Avoid gloves near spinning tools.

Safe Practices

- Choose stabilized woods when possible. They are more dimensionally stable and typically safer to work than raw wood or exotics.

- Always sand with dust collection and a respirator. Even if you cannot see it, the fine dust is there.

- Wash hands after handling exotic woods, even if you wore gloves. Some oils persist.

- Keep medical awareness. If you start coughing, wheezing, or develop rashes while working a wood, stop immediately. Repeated exposure will only worsen symptoms.

- Avoid working woods near open flames or hot equipment. Fine dust can ignite.

- Store woods in controlled humidity (40–60 percent relative humidity) to minimize warping and cracking.

- Clearly label exotic wood blocks so you remember which are high-risk species.

- If you have asthma, keep an inhaler nearby and never work wood without proper ventilation.

> Your brain is the most important tool in the shop. Don't leave it at home.

Disposal Considerations

- Bag sanding dust before disposal to prevent it from spreading.

- Do not burn exotic wood dust. Many release toxic fumes when burned.

- Larger scraps may be kept for liners or small projects, but avoid hoarding splinter bins.

- Stabilized wood offcuts and dust should go in sealed bags to landfill.

Practical Shop Notes

- Keep a reference list of wood toxicity (many are published online or in woodworking safety guides). There is a general chart in the reference materials section.

- Stabilization makes woods stabler, but not dust-free. Always wear PPE.

- Store exotic wood dust separately in sealed bags or bins to reduce shop-wide exposure.

- In most shops, use a shop air purifier in addition to personal respirators when sanding.

- If you notice recurring symptoms after working with a certain species, stop using it. No project is worth permanent lung damage or skin irritation.

Working alone is fine until it isn't.

Section 4.2 – Handle Preparation & Fitting

Before a handle becomes something smooth and comfortable in the hand, it begins as a block of raw material. It is square, rough, and often uncooperative. The process of preparing that block into usable scales or a fitted hidden-tang handle is one of the most important and most underestimated steps in knife making. This is the point where your handle stops being a chunk of material and starts becoming part of a tool. If preparation is sloppy, the rest of the build is doomed. You will fight gaps, crooked alignment, or pin holes that never quite line up. Handle prep is not glamorous. There are no sparks flying, no fire burning, no dramatic plunge into oil. Instead, it is about patience, measuring twice, drilling once, and paying attention to the details. But just because it is calmer does not mean it is safer. In fact, this stage often hides hazards in plain sight. Small pieces of material, awkward to hold, meet fast-moving saw blades, drill bits, and clamps. All it takes is one slip for a block to split, a drill bit to grab, or a tang corner to slice skin during a careless dry fit. Many makers learn these lessons the hard way. A set of scales clamped by hand on a drill press suddenly spinning like a propeller. A block splitting clean in two because a pilot hole was skipped. Or worse, rushing to test-fit the tang and realizing too late that a sharp edge did not care whether the knife was finished or not. What is supposed to be a simple step can quickly send you searching for bandages.

The truth is, good handle prep is like laying a foundation for a house. Nobody admires the concrete footings, but if they are crooked or cracked, the whole structure suffers. Care here pays dividends later. Cleaner glue-ups, tighter joints, less wasted material, and safer shaping. More importantly, it keeps you from treating your fingers like collateral damage along the way.

Major Hazards

Cutting & Squaring

- Splinters and chips when sawing blocks to size.
- Kickback or binding when cutting small pieces on band saws or scroll saws.

Drilling & Slotting

- Drill bits grabbing material and spinning it unexpectedly.
- Scales splitting during drilling if unsupported.
- Burrs on holes creating sharp edges.

Clamping & Dry Fitting

- Workpieces shifting or launching from improper clamping.
- Tang or blade edges cutting hands during trial fits.

> Mental health days aren't a weakness. They're maintenance.

General Risks

- Mishandling tools due to working with small, awkwardly sized pieces.

- Rushing prep work, leading to poor alignment and repeated rework.

PPE

- Safety Glasses: always during cutting and drilling. Chips travel fast.

- Respirator: especially when drilling stabilized woods, Micarta, or G10.

- Gloves (Selective Use): nitrile gloves for handling oily or tropical woods. Avoid bulky gloves near saws or drill presses.

- Hearing Protection: sanders, lathes, and rotary tools produce high sustained noise.

Safe Practices

Squaring Material

- Always check the material for defects (cracks, voids, knots) before cutting. Defects often catch blades and can throw pieces unexpectedly.

- When cutting small handle blocks, use a sled or miter gauge rather than pushing pieces freehand against a fence. This prevents binding and kickback.

- Push sticks or push blocks keep hands away from saw blades when cutting down smaller scales or spacers.

Drilling Holes

- Clamp every piece. A drill press vise, quick-grip clamps, or even a sacrificial backing board with hold-downs should always be used. A hand-held piece can spin violently the moment the bit grabs.

- For scales, tape them together (book-matched) and drill both at once. This ensures better pin hole alignment and reduces the risk of splitting one scale when drilling them separately.

- Use sharp bits and appropriate speeds. Dull bits cause heat buildup, increasing the chance of splitting or glazing resin in stabilized woods.

- Back up the piece with a sacrificial board to prevent blowout and reduce the risk of chipped or jagged hole exits.

- Remove burrs immediately with a deburring tool, file, or sandpaper. Those razor edges cut more fingers than the blade itself at this stage.

If you're too tired to focus, you're too tired to be in the shop.

Tang Slotting (Hidden Tang Knives)

- When drilling a tang slot, always drill undersized holes first and then carefully square them with chisels, broach, or file. Oversized slots lead to poor fit and wasted material.

- If using a mill or rotary tool, secure the block tightly and move slowly. Forcing the tool often causes chatter, which can crack the block.

- Avoid overheating stabilized woods and antlers while slotting. Prolonged friction can soften resin or char organic materials.

Dry Fitting & Alignment

- Tape sharp edges of the tang and blade before test fits to prevent accidental cuts.

- Always check pin alignment with dry-fit pins before mixing epoxy. A fraction of a millimeter off can lock the handle into misalignment once glued.

- Apply light pressure with soft clamps (spring clamps or padded C-clamps) to hold test assemblies together without crushing delicate wood assemblies.

- Perform alignment checks under bright, even light. Shadows and poor lighting can trick your eye into thinking a gap is not there.

General Work Mindset

- Treat every step like it is permanent. Rushing through prep often means re-drilling or re-cutting, which either destroys or weakens both the material and your patience.

- Keep the work area clear of clutter when prepping. Handle blocks are small, and a stray scrap or tool on the drill press table is all it takes to tilt a workpiece into a dangerous bind.

- Respect small size. The smaller the piece, the greater the hazard. If a block or spacer is too small to clamp securely, do not risk it. Glue it to a larger sacrificial board first for safe handling.

Disposal Considerations

- Collect sawdust and chips as you go to avoid slipping hazards.

- Small scraps from squaring can be saved for spacers, but discard anything too small to be safely clamped later.

- Bag fine dust from stabilized woods or synthetics separately for disposal.

> "I'll just finish this one thing" is how most accidents start.

Practical Shop Notes

- Keep a dedicated drill press vise for handle blocks and scales. It saves fingers.

- Use painters tape to mark alignment on both tang and scales before drilling.

- Test-fit pins dry before mixing epoxy. Discovering misalignment during glue-up is a nightmare.

- Keep a small brush or compressed air handy to clear chips between drilling passes.

Your body keeps score. Listen to it before it starts yelling.

Section 4.3 – Woodworking Tools for Handle Making

Once your handle material is squared, drilled, and ready, the real shaping begins. This is the point where a block of wood, Micarta, or G10 starts to look like a knife handle rather than just another shop offcut. Bandsaws, scroll saws, rasps, files, chisels, and sanders all come into play. Each has the ability to turn a chunk of material into something ergonomic, elegant, and functional. These tools are precise and capable. But they are also some of the most deceptively hazardous in the shop. The reason comes down to scale. In cabinetmaking or carpentry, you are often cutting boards several feet long. These give you room to stabilize and keep your hands clear. Knife handles, by contrast, are small, awkward, and unforgiving. A two-inch block does not leave much margin for error when it meets a band saw blade. A thin scale can twist, bind, or catch in an instant. A belt sander may smooth one moment and launch your piece across the shop the next. Tools that are safe with furniture-sized stock suddenly become something else entirely when you are working with handle-scale material. Ask any experienced knifemaker, and they will have a story. The belt sander that grabbed a scale and flung it across the room like a throwing star. The rasp that slipped and left a gouge in a palm instead of the wood. Or the scroll saw blade that snapped under too much pressure. These are not catastrophic, headline-making accidents. But they are the kinds of small injuries that add up. Stitches, bandaged fingers, ruined workpieces. The real lesson is that woodworking tools are not inherently dangerous. But handle work pushes them into conditions where extra caution is needed. You are often holding pieces closer to the blade than you would like. You are applying pressure on shapes that do not sit flat. Or you are sanding edges thinner than they were ever meant to be. Respecting the limitations of both the tool and the material is what keeps your fingers safe and your handle intact.

This section will look at each of the most common woodworking tools used in handle making. It covers the hazards unique to them and the safe practices that keep the process efficient and blood-free.

Major Hazards

Bandsaws & Scroll Saws

- Fingers too close to the blade when cutting small pieces.
- Workpieces binding or twisting into the blade.
- Blade breakage if forcing cuts.

Belt & Disc Sanders

- Workpieces launched if caught at the wrong angle.
- Heat buildup causing burns on fingers.
- Dust hazards from wood, Micarta, or G10.

> The shop is patient. It will wait until you get lazy.

Rasps, Files & Chisels

- Slips causing hand or finger injuries.

- Splinters from aggressive cuts.

- Chisels breaking or chipping under heavy force.

Note: Remember the old carpenter's saying. A dull chisel is the most dangerous tool in the woodshop. Dull tools demand force, and force leads to slips.

General Hazards

- Awkward grip on small pieces leading to loss of control.

- Excessive force causing tools to dig in and jump.

- Dust accumulation from extended shaping.

PPE

- Safety Glasses or Face Shield: to guard against flying chips or pieces.

- Respirator: especially with synthetic handle materials or exotic woods.

- Hearing Protection: sanders and saws generate sustained high noise levels.

- Gloves (Limited Use): work gloves for hand-tool work like rasps, but never around power-driven tools.

Safe Practices

Bandsaws & Scroll Saws

- Always use a push stick or jig when cutting small pieces.

- Keep hands to the side of the blade's path. Never directly behind the cut.

- Do not force the cut. Let the blade do the work.

- Inspect blades for cracks or wear before use.

Belt & Disc Sanders

- Present workpieces gently, with steady pressure.

- Keep fingers clear. Sanders generate heat quickly, and hot wood can burn skin on contact.

- Sand at the correct angle to prevent the piece from catching and flying.

- Use dust collection and empty bags often. Fine dust builds up fast.

Safety is the only thing that lets you keep making knives tomorrow.

Rasps, Files & Chisels

- Always cut away from your body and hands.

- Keep edges sharp. Dull tools demand force and slip more easily.

- Secure the workpiece in a vise whenever possible.

- Do not pry with chisels. They are made for cutting, not leverage.

General Practices

- Work with good lighting so you can see your cuts clearly.

- Take breaks. Fatigue increases the chance of slips.

- Keep tools sharp and clean. Sharp edges are safer than dull ones.

- Respect the size of your workpiece. If it is too small to safely cut, secure it to something larger.

Disposal Considerations

- Collect sawdust from sanding frequently. It accumulates faster than you think.

- Bag fine dust separately, especially if working with stabilized or composite materials.

- Store broken blades in a dedicated container to avoid puncture hazards in the trash.

Practical Shop Notes

- Keep a small-bin dust collector or shop vac near sanding stations.

- Invest in fine rasps or micro-rasps. They give control where power tools are too risky.

- A scroll saw can be safer than a bandsaw for delicate handle curves.

- Keep a spray bottle of water nearby to cool down hot workpieces.

That pile of scrap metal is not storage. It's a foot guillotine.

Section 4.4 – Adhesives & Bonding Agents in Handle Work

Adhesives are the quiet force that holds a knife handle together. Mechanical fasteners, pins, bolts, or rivets may provide visible strength, but it is often the glue beneath the surface that decides whether a handle lasts a lifetime or begins to fail after a few months of use. In most modern knife making adhesives are not optional, they are essential. Epoxies remain the standard. They are valued for their unmatched strength and ability to bond dissimilar materials. But epoxies are only one part of the adhesive family. Cyanoacrylates, also known as CA or superglues, fill gaps, seal porous wood, and tack things in place in seconds. Accelerants are used to push CA glues to instant hardness but at the cost of harsh chemical vapors. Wood glues still play a role when laminating certain liners or joining non-critical wooden components. Metal-filled compounds like JB Weld offer reinforcement when needed. Every adhesive brings unique advantages, but also unique hazards. Epoxy carries the risk of permanent skin sensitization and lung irritation from dust once cured. CA glue bonds skin as effectively as it bonds handle material and releases vapors that sting eyes and lungs. Wood glues, though milder, still present issues when sanded or overheated. JB Weld can introduce heavy-metal exposure concerns, while expanding urethane glues can push joints apart instead of pulling them together if misused. Understanding adhesives means more than just knowing which one to reach for. It means knowing how to handle them safely, how to store them correctly, and how to dispose of them responsibly. Used wisely, they are the unseen strength of a well-made knife. Used carelessly, they can compromise your work, your shop environment, and even your health.

This section outlines the different adhesives most commonly encountered in knife making, their hazards, the protective measures that should always accompany them, and the practical steps that keep them as allies instead of liabilities.

Major Hazards by Adhesive

Epoxy (2-part resins & hardeners)

- Strongest bond for handle scales and hidden tangs.

- Hazards: chemical burns, skin sensitization, fumes, dust when sanding cured epoxy.

The lathe doesn't want to be your friend. It wants your sleeve.

Cyanoacrylate (CA / Superglue)

- Great for quick fixes, small gaps, and sealing porous woods.

- Great for workholding small parts.

- Hazards:

    o   bonds skin instantly.

    o   fumes irritate eyes and lungs.

    o   accelerants create strong chemical vapors.

- Risk of exothermic reaction (heat) when used with cotton or paper.

Wood Glue (PVA & aliphatic resin glues)

- Safer option for liner laminations, wooden spacers, or non-structural applications.

- Hazards: less toxic, but sanding dried glue produces irritating dust

- Poor water resistance unless using specialized outdoor formulations.

JB Weld & Metal-Filled Epoxies

- Used for metal-to-metal or heavy-duty fixes. Occasionally for guard or pommel work.

- Hazards: same as epoxy, with additional heavy-metal exposure risks from fillers.

Other Specialty Adhesives (urethane glues, hot melts, etc.)

- Less common, but each carries unique risks.

- Urethane glues expand aggressively

- Hot melts can burn skin.

PPE

- Gloves: nitrile (essential for epoxies, CA, and JB Weld). Avoid cotton. CA glue reacts dangerously with it.

- Respirator: organic vapor cartridges for liquid adhesives. P100 filters when sanding cured glue.

- Eye Protection: goggles or sealed glasses for splash-prone adhesives like CA and epoxy.

- Ventilation: always use adhesives in a well-ventilated space. Fans or fume extractors are strongly recommended.

Your first aid kit is the only thing that still likes you in this shop.

Safe Practices

Epoxies

- Mix in small batches. Large pours overheat quickly.

- Follow the manufacturer's ratio precisely.

- Never touch epoxy bare-handed. Sensitization is permanent and irreversible.

- Sand only when fully cured. Capture dust at the source.

CA Glues (Superglues)

- Apply in small amounts. Excess makes brittle joints.

- Avoid using cotton or cloth. The reaction creates heat and can burn.

- Use accelerants sparingly. Fumes are potent.

- Keep acetone nearby for emergency skin release.

Wood Glues

- Clamp pieces tightly and allow full cure. Rushing causes joint failure.

- Avoid skin contact. Though mild, long-term exposure can still cause dermatitis.

- Clean squeeze-out immediately. Sanding it later releases fine dust that can irritate skin and lungs.

JB Weld / Metal-Filled Adhesives

- Wear gloves at all times. Fillers can contain hazardous metals.

- Mix thoroughly. Improper ratios cause weak bonds.

- Dispose of cured leftovers properly. Do not leave liquid material open on benches.

General Adhesive Rules

- Label bottles with purchase date. Adhesives have shelf lives.

- Store upright, sealed tightly, at room temperature.

- Keep away from heat sources. Many adhesives are flammable.

- Never mix brands or types. Unpredictable reactions can occur.

The extension cord across the floor is not a decoration. It's a trap.

Disposal Considerations

- Fully cured adhesives (epoxies, CA, JB Weld, wood glues) can usually go in regular trash.

- Liquid leftovers should be treated as hazardous. Check local regulations.

- Never pour adhesives down drains.

- Collect contaminated rags in sealed, fire-safe containers.

Practical Shop Notes

- Keep a small stash of single-use epoxy packs for small jobs. They reduce waste and mess.

- Store CA glue in the fridge (in a sealed container) to extend shelf life.

- Use painter's tape around joints before glue-up to minimize cleanup (when appropriate).

- Always test adhesives on scrap before committing to a handle.

- Keep plenty of paper towels and acetone or denatured alcohol nearby during glue-ups.

Kids treat your shop like an interactive museum called "Touch Everything."

Section 4.5 – Shaping & Finishing Handles

Shaping and finishing is where all of the groundwork comes together. Up until this stage, the handle has looked like a blocky assembly of glued scales, pins, and epoxy. Now, the excess disappears, the lines emerge, and the knife finally begins to feel like something you can hold and use. For many makers, this is the most enjoyable part of the build. Watching raw material transform into smooth contours and polished surfaces is satisfying. It is also the point where the artistry of knife making shines through: curves appear, edges crisp, and the handle finally feels alive in the hand. But shaping and finishing are also where many projects go wrong. Unlike forging or grinding, where mistakes are usually obvious, errors at this stage can be subtle. Remove just a fraction too much material, and you create uncomfortable contours or expose the tang. Rush through sanding, and scratches that were invisible at 80 grit suddenly glare at you under polish. Buff too aggressively, and you may lose control of the entire knife. Impatience is the silent hazard here, leading to ruined work or worse, injuries. The tools do not make this stage safer, either. Belt sanders, disc sanders, and buffers are all capable of grabbing a handle and flinging it across the shop faster than you can react. Even simple hand sanding has its risks: repetitive strain, splinters, and hours of dust exposure if you neglect PPE. Finishing compounds add another layer of risk: oils, waxes, and cyanoacrylate coatings can all irritate skin or release harmful vapors. Even oily rags left in a pile can spontaneously ignite.

This stage is the final test of your discipline. The temptation is to relax because the knife looks almost done. In reality, shaping and finishing require the same focus and respect for safety as forging or grinding. The reward for care and patience is a handle that not only looks beautiful but feels comfortable in the hand, a handle that will last. The punishment for rushing is often a project that is forever compromised or, worse, an injury that overshadows the satisfaction of your work.

Major Hazards

Power Tools (Grinders, Sanders, Buffers)

- Belts grabbing workpieces and throwing them.
- Heat buildup burning wood or scorching stabilized materials.
- Buffers catching edges and launching knives.
- Hearing damage from prolonged exposure.
- Scrapes and cuts from complacency.

The grinder is hungry. Don't volunteer to be lunch.

Hand Tools (Files, Rasps, Sandpaper)

- Slips leading to cuts or gouges.

- Repetitive strain injuries from extended hand sanding.

- Splinters from unfinished wood edges.

Dust & Chemicals

- Fine particulate dust from wood, stabilized materials, or adhesives.

- Fumes from finishes such as oils, waxes, or cyanoacrylate coatings.

General Hazards

- Removing too much material too quickly.

- Working without proper PPE, especially during finishing.

- Complacency

PPE

- Safety Glasses or Face Shield: absolutely essential when sanding or buffing.

- Respirator: P100 filters during sanding; organic vapor cartridges when applying finishes.

- Gloves (Selective): work gloves when hand sanding or filing raw wood, but never near moving belts or buffers.

- Hearing Protection: sanders, grinders, and buffers all produce high sustained noise.

Safe Practices

Shaping with Power Tools

- Use light, controlled pressure. Let the tool do the work.

- Keep handles away from belt edges that can catch.

- Frequently cool material with water to avoid overheating wood or resin.

- Never use gloves near rotating belts or buffers.

- Use sharp belts and blades to alleviate excessive friction.

Your apron smells like bacon for a reason. That reason is you.

Hand Shaping & Sanding

- Secure the knife in a vise or clamp before filing or sanding.
- Always sand with the grain where possible to prevent tear-out.
- Switch grits progressively. Skipping grits leads to frustration and poor finishes.
- Take breaks to prevent hand fatigue and repetitive strain.
- Protect sharp edges from inadvertent contact.

Finishing Applications

- Apply oils, waxes, or sealants in well-ventilated areas.
- Use clean, lint-free cloths for applying finishes. CA glue and accelerants with cotton can cause burns.
- Allow proper cure time before handling or buffing finished handles.
- Dispose of oily rags in a sealed metal container to prevent spontaneous combustion.

Final Buffing & Polishing

- Use extreme caution. Buffers are notorious for injuries.
- Always keep the wheel turning away from edges, not into them.
- Hold firmly but never force the knife. Let the wheel do the polishing.
- Stay clear of the launch zone directly below the wheel in case the knife is caught.
- Be aware of sharp edges and protect them as necessary.

Disposal Considerations

- Collect sanding dust regularly. Exotic dust can remain in the air long after cleanup.
- Dispose of used sandpaper and rags immediately.
- Oily rags can ignite spontaneously.
- Keep solvent-soaked rags in sealed, fire-safe containers.

Practical Shop Notes

- Keep your files and rasps sharp. Sharp tools cut cleaner and safer than dull ones.
- Work up through grits slowly. Finishing starts at 80 grit, not 400.
- A light mist of water on sandpaper helps with stabilized woods, keeping dust down and surfaces smooth.
- Always check fit against your hand during shaping. Comfort matters as much as appearance.

The shop doesn't do participation trophies. It does Darwin Awards.

Section 4.6 – Finishing & Sealing

Finishing and sealing is often the last step before a knife leaves the shop, and it carries more weight than many makers realize. Shaping brings a handle to form, but finishing gives it permanence. It is the stage that decides whether the knife will remain comfortable and resilient after years of use or begin to break down the moment it meets sweat, water, and dirt in the real world. A good finish protects the handle from moisture, stabilizes the surface against wear, and enhances the natural beauty of the wood or synthetic material. But this final stage is often overlooked in terms of safety. The tools may be quieter and the work less dramatic, yet the risks are real. Finishes like boiled linseed oil or tung oil can irritate the skin, and the rags used to apply them can ignite hours after being tossed in the trash. Synthetic sealants release fumes that linger in the lungs. Cyanoacrylate finishes can bond skin faster than they harden on wood. Even waxes, seemingly harmless, can become hazards when applied near open flames or hot tools. Finishing requires more than simply wiping on a coat of oil. It demands patience, careful application, and the discipline to let materials cure fully before moving on. Rushing this process almost always backfires. Sticky surfaces that never fully dry, blotchy finishes that cloud the grain, or in the worst cases, smoldering rags left to start a shop fire. It is not the stage to relax or cut corners, even if the knife looks nearly complete.

Handled properly, finishing is both protective and artistic. It seals the handle against time and use while showcasing the craftsmanship invested in shaping it. Done poorly, it can undermine both the knife's longevity and the maker's safety. Respecting the materials, following best practices, and giving finishes the time they require is what separates a rushed project from a lasting piece of work.

Major Hazards

Chemical Exposure

- Fumes from oils, waxes, and synthetic finishes.
- Skin irritation from prolonged contact.
- Risk of allergic reactions to natural oils (for example, tung oil, linseed oil).

Fire Hazards

- Rags soaked in drying oils (boiled linseed, tung oil) can spontaneously combust.
- Heat sources near flammable solvents or waxes increase fire risk.

"I'll just do one more pass" is how most fingers file for unemployment.

Application Risks

- Over-applying finishes leads to sticky, uneven surfaces.

- Using accelerants or heat guns improperly can cause burns or fire.

- Handling knives too soon after finishing risks smearing or chemical burns.

PPE

- Respirator: organic vapor cartridges for oil, wax, or synthetic finishes.

- Gloves: nitrile gloves to prevent skin absorption.

- Eye Protection: safety glasses when applying sprays or wiping liquids.

- Apron or Protective Clothing: avoid ruined clothes or accidental skin exposure.

Safe Practices

Application

- Apply in thin, even coats. Excess finish rarely adds durability.

- Follow manufacturer's directions for drying and re-coating times.

- Use clean, lint-free cloths or applicators to prevent contamination.

- Always work in a well-ventilated space. Outdoors if possible.

Drying & Curing

- Place finished knives on a stable, dust-free rack while drying.

- Allow full cure before polishing or handling to avoid surface damage.

- Do not rush drying with open flame or high heat sources.

Handling Rags & Applicators

- Spread dirty rags flat outdoors to dry before disposal.

- Store used rags or applicators in a sealed, fire-safe container until cured.

- Never leave piles of oily rags unattended in the shop.

Sealing Options

- Oils (linseed, tung, mineral oil): enhance grain and provide water resistance.

- Waxes (beeswax, carnauba): add sheen and protection but need reapplication.

- Cyanoacrylate (CA finishes): provide hard, durable surfaces but release heavy fumes.

- Synthetic coatings (polyurethane, epoxy sealants): offer strong protection but require careful application.

Disposal Considerations

- Treat uncured rags, brushes, and excess finish as hazardous waste.

- Fully cured oils, waxes, or sealants are generally safe to discard in normal trash.

- Check local regulations for solvent-based finishes. Some require special disposal.

Practical Shop Notes

- Warm oils slightly (if possible) before use to improve penetration.

- Keep a dedicated finishing area separate from grinding and sanding dust.

- Label all finishes clearly. Some look nearly identical but behave very differently.

- Keep records of what finish was used on each knife for consistency and customer care instructions.

Your shop vacuum is basically a fire starter with a fancy hose.

Section 4.7 – Wood Turning & Specialty Handle Work

Not every knife handle stops at flat scales and clean shaping. Some knives call for something more. Curves formed on a lathe, intricate inlays of shell or stone, textured grips that improve function, or decorative burns and carvings that showcase artistry. These are the touches that separate a working knife from a custom piece. They are what give a knife personality, and they are often what draw a buyer's eye first. Specialty work like wood turning, inlays, texturing, or pyrography is not necessary for every project, but when done well, it turns a finished tool into a statement. This type of creativity brings complexity, and complexity brings risk. Wood lathes spin blocks at hundreds or even thousands of revolutions per minute, and a poorly secured blank can become a missile in a heartbeat. Carving and texturing involve working close to the material with sharp hand tools where slips often mean stitches. Inlays use shell, stone, metal, or more. Each produces hazardous dusts and chips when cut. Wood burning creates fumes that are as harmful to your lungs as epoxy dust, though it smells deceptively pleasant at first. The attraction of specialty work is its freedom. No two handles will ever look exactly the same. But that freedom comes with fewer guidelines, less predictability, and the need for a heightened sense of discipline. A lathe does not forgive hesitation, and a wood burner does not care if your hand drifts an inch too far. Just as with forging or grinding, the hazards here are real. Only quieter and sometimes easier to ignore.

Specialty handle work is where craftsmanship and artistry meet safety and patience. It is where the maker's personal voice shines through, but also where overconfidence or carelessness can undo hours of progress in an instant. With the right respect for the tools, the materials, and the hazards, specialty work can become the most rewarding and most distinctive part of the knife-making process.

Major Hazards

Wood Turning (Lathes)

- Workpieces coming loose and ejecting at high speed.

- Tools catching and jerking suddenly.

- Dust exposure from continuous cutting.

Carving, Filing & Texturing

- Slips leading to deep cuts.

- Awkward hand positions near sharp tools.

- Strain from repetitive, detailed work.

The forge doesn't care if you're tired. It still wants to burn you.

Wood Burning & Pyrography

- Fumes from burning wood or finishes.

- Burns from hot pens or tips.

- Fire hazards from poor ventilation or flammable surfaces.

Inlays (Metal, Shell, Stone)

- Dust inhalation from shell or stone (for example, mother-of-pearl is especially hazardous).

- Metal filings irritate eyes and skin.

- Tiny workpieces breaking or flying under tool pressure.

PPE

- Safety Glasses or Face Shield: essential for wood turning and inlay work.

- Respirator: P100 or equivalent for fine dust, especially shell, stone, or burnt wood.

- Gloves (Selective): avoid spinning lathes, but thin gloves can help during carving.

- Hearing Protection: lathes, rotary tools, and carving stations can be loud.

Safe Practices

Wood Turning

- Always check that the blank is securely mounted before starting.

- Stand out of the direct line of fire when first starting the lathe.

- Use sharp tools to avoid catches. Dull edges are unpredictable.

- Keep tool rests close to the workpiece and adjust often.

- Never wear gloves, jewelry, or loose clothing near a spinning lathe.

- Use the appropriate lathe speed for the size and type of material. Start at lower speeds with unbalanced or irregular blanks.

- Know the location of your emergency stop or how to quickly shut down the lathe in case of a catch or ejection.

Carving & Texturing

- Always cut away from your body, never toward it.

- Secure the part in a vise or jig before carving details.

- Take frequent breaks. Fatigue leads to slips.

- Keep carving knives razor sharp. Dull edges require more force.

That "quick fix" usually ends with a long recovery and a good story.

Wood Burning / Pyrography

- Work only in a well-ventilated space or under a fume extractor.

- Keep burning tools on heat-proof stands when not in use.

- Never leave hot burners unattended.

- Avoid burning woods with unknown finishes or stabilizers. The fumes can be toxic.

Inlays

- Wear a respirator when cutting or sanding shell, stone, or mother-of-pearl.

- Cut small pieces slowly and with the correct blades or burrs to prevent shattering.

- Use magnification when working with tiny inlay parts to reduce eye strain and mistakes.

- Test-fit before gluing. Inlays are unforgiving once set.

Disposal Considerations

- Collect wood dust and chips regularly, especially from turning.

- Store shell and stone dust separately and dispose of as hazardous waste where required.

- Allow wood burning tips and tools to cool fully before storage.

Practical Shop Notes

- Keep a dedicated dust collector or shop vac on lathes. Turning produces lots of scrap and continuous fine dust.

- Use calipers often when turning. It is easy to remove too much material.

- Test decorative burns or textures on scrap before committing to a handle.

- Keep inlay materials organized in small containers. They are easy to lose.

Note: Specialty work is slow work. Patience is as much a tool as the chisel.

Complacency is silent. The ER is not.

First Aid & Emergency Response

Working in a knife shop or metalworking environment means living with the constant possibility of injury. Sparks fly, tools bite, chemicals splash, and sometimes fatigue or distraction gets the better of even the most experienced maker. No matter how careful you are, accidents happen. That is why first aid and emergency response are not just nice-to-know skills. They are essential survival tools. This section is not written to frighten you. It is here to prepare you. Because when things go wrong in the shop, they go wrong fast. The middle of an emergency is the worst time to start searching for what to do for a bad burn, or whatever the issue is. First aid is about more than bandages and antiseptic. It is about keeping a small injury from becoming a big one, buying time until professionals can step in, and having a plan when chaos erupts. Your shop, whether it is a garage, shed, or small business workspace, is not designed to save lives. The nearest emergency room may be fifteen minutes away, or much longer if you are rural. That makes your first line of response critical. A rag wrapped around a bleeding hand may not be ideal, but it is better than bleeding out. A quick rinse of an eye may prevent permanent blindness. Knowing when to call 911 can save your life or the life of someone working with you. Think of this chapter as your survival kit for shop injuries. It does not replace professional medical care, but it does help you bridge the gap between injury and treatment. The single most dangerous assumption in a shop is, it will not happen to me. Every knifemaker who has worked long enough can tell stories of burns, cuts, chemical splashes, or worse. In almost every story, the difference between recovery and tragedy comes down to how quickly and how well the injury was handled in the first minutes. That is why this section emphasizes preparedness. Stocking a first aid kit that goes beyond a few dusty band-aids. Posting emergency contacts where anyone can find them. Training yourself and others around you to respond without hesitation. Talking with your spouse, family, or neighbors about what to look for when you come stumbling in from the shop holding your hand, arm, or head. Preparation is not paranoia. It is insurance. It is acknowledging that the shop, for all its creativity and satisfaction, is also full of hazards. This section will give you practical steps for the most common emergencies you may face in the shop. You will learn first aid basics, including how to stock, organize, and use your kit. It explains burns, both thermal and electrical, and how to cool, protect, and treat them. You will find guidance on cuts and lacerations, including how to control bleeding and prevent infection. Eye and respiratory injuries are covered, with clear instructions on flushing, protecting, and knowing when to seek help. Chemical burns and exposures receive detailed attention, showing what to do when acids, solvents, or adhesives contact skin or eyes.

First Aid & Emergency Response

The buffer is silent until it decides today is the day it plays fastball.

Emergency contacts and planning are included so help is always within reach. Finally, the last section addresses head injuries and concussions, helping you recognize the hidden dangers of what may seem like just a bump. When something happens, panic is your enemy. Blood looks worse than it is. Burns hurt more than they heal. Head injuries make you want to argue instead of listen. The key is to slow down, take a breath, and work the problem. One of the recurring themes you will see in this section is that you are rarely the best judge of your own condition after an injury. You may be in shock, confused, or determined to push through. That is where others come in: spouses, family members, neighbors, coworkers, or apprentices. They may notice you are acting strangely after a head injury. They may insist on calling 911 when you are stubbornly refusing. They may be the ones applying pressure to your wound while you sit down and stop fighting. That is why part of your preparation is having conversations with them before anything happens. Let them know where your first aid kit is. Tell them what to do if you pass out. Give them permission to ignore your "I am fine" routine.

You spend hours making knives, tuning machines, and planning projects. Spend a little time sharpening your emergency plan as well. First aid in the shop is not optional. It is the safety net under everything else you do. It does not just protect your hands or your eyes; it protects your future as a maker. And remember: nothing slows down your work and empties your wallet faster than a trip to the emergency room. But when that trip is unavoidable, the steps you take in the shop before you arrive can make all the difference.

Stubbornness is not a safety feature.

Section 5.1 – Basic First Aid in the Shop

Even the most careful knifemaker will eventually need first aid. The shop is full of hazards. Sharp edges, spinning belts, hot steel, dust that irritates lungs and eyes, and chemicals that burn or sensitize skin are everywhere. It is a place where prevention is always the first goal, but preparedness must be the backup. Injuries do not have to be catastrophic to matter. A splinter, a small cut, or a fingertip nick may seem minor, but every one of them is still an injury. Left untreated, these little insults can slow you down, become infected, or in the worst cases turn into something that keeps you out of the shop entirely. Knifemakers often joke that band-aids are part of the uniform, but the truth is that first aid deserves more respect. A sloppy bandage or worse, ignoring the injury altogether, can lead to repeat trauma, infection, or contamination of your work. Hot metal does not care that you cut your finger earlier, and grinders do not pause just because you already have one bandage on. Treating injuries promptly and properly is what keeps small problems small instead of allowing them to pile up into big ones. Being prepared with the right supplies is what makes that possible. Too many shops rely on a half-empty box of mismatched band-aids and a bottle of hydrogen peroxide that expired a decade ago. A knife shop needs a dedicated, well-stocked kit designed around the hazards of the trade. Gauze pads, roller wraps, burn gel, eye wash, tweezers, and yes multiple types of band-aids all belong in that kit. Knowing how to use them is just as important as having them because in the moment of an accident hesitation wastes time you may not have.

First aid in the shop is not about making you invincible. It is about managing injuries effectively so you can return to your work safely without compounding the damage. It is also about recognizing when to stop and seek professional help. Pride and stubbornness have kept more than one maker working through an injury that later landed them in the ER. Respecting first aid is part of respecting yourself as a craftsman.

First Aid Kit – What It Should Include

Your kit should go beyond a few band-aids. Think about the specific hazards of a knife shop and prepare accordingly.

Bleeding Control

- Sterile Gauze Pads: For covering and absorbing blood.

- Roller Gauze / Kling Wrap: For holding pads in place and applying pressure.

- Pressure Bandages: For serious bleeding control.

- Tourniquet: Last resort for heavy bleeding. Know how to use it properly.

- Adhesive Bandages (multiple types): Not all band-aids are the same. Stock fingertip bandages, knuckle bandages, large flexible strips, and waterproof styles.

Coffee is not a substitute for sleep.

Note: In an emergency, a clean shop rag and tape are better than bleeding out, but proper sterile gauze is always best.

Burn Care

- Burn Gel or Burn Dressing: For immediate cooling of minor to moderate burns.
- Cold Packs: For reducing pain and swelling.
- Non-stick Dressings: To cover burns without sticking to damaged skin.

Eye & Respiratory

- Eye Wash Bottles / Saline Solution: For flushing dust, grit, or chemicals.
- Eye Cups or Station: Mounted in the shop, easy to find.
- Emergency Breathing Mask: For assisting someone who has inhaled fumes or dust.

Splinters & Small Foreign Bodies

- Tweezers (pointed and flat): Sterile, not your shop knife.
- Magnifying Glass or Headlamp: For precise removal.
- Alcohol Wipes: To clean before and after removal.

Chemicals & Adhesives

- Gloves (Nitrile): For handling chemical exposure.
- pH Neutralizer / Flush (if applicable): For specific shop chemicals, check safety sheets.

General Supplies

- Medical Tape (hypoallergenic)
- Elastic Wrap Bandages
- Scissors (dedicated to first aid, not your shop scissors)
- CPR Mask or Shield
- Emergency Blanket (shock, cold, or burns)
- First Aid Manual / Quick Guide

The shop will still be here tomorrow. You might not be if you push it.

Safe Practices in First Aid

Cuts & Lacerations

- Clean with antiseptic wipes or clean water.
- Apply gauze and pressure until bleeding stops.
- Cover with sterile bandages.
- Protect the wound before returning to work. A band-aid is only effective if it stays on, shields against dirt, and prevents reopening.

Burns

- Cool immediately under running water for at least 10 minutes.
- Do not use oils, butter, or random "remedies."
- Apply burn gel or non-stick dressing.

Eye Injuries

- Flush continuously with saline or clean water for at least 15 minutes.
- Do not rub the eye.
- Seek medical attention if pain persists or a foreign object is embedded.

Splinters

- Clean the area first.
- Use sterilized tweezers, not sharp blades.
- Cover with a small bandage after removal.

Serious Injuries

- Call emergency services immediately.
- Apply a tourniquet only if bleeding cannot be controlled with pressure.
- Do not hesitate. Time matters.

Note: Each of these injury types will be covered in greater detail in the following subsections of Section 5. This overview is about basic preparedness and response.

Basic First Aid in the Shop

First Aid Kit – Where it should be located

The best first aid kit in the world is useless if you cannot reach it in seconds when you need it. In a knife shop every second counts. OSHA 1910.151 requires that first aid supplies be "readily available," and ANSI Z308.1 reinforces that kits must be placed where they can be accessed immediately without obstacles. Here is the practical reality for a maker's shop.

- Mount the main kit on the wall in a central, highly visible spot near your primary workbench so you can grab it in three steps or less.

- Keep it within 10-15 seconds' reach from any major work area: the grinder, forge, or bandsaw station.

- Place it near an exit or by the shop phone so you can get supplies and call for help at the same time.

- Use large, bold lettering and the universal red-cross symbol so anyone walking into the shop (kids, visitors, or your spouse) can spot it instantly.

- Hang the kit at eye level or slightly lower. High enough to stay out of the way, low enough to reach even if you are already hurt.

- Keep the area directly in front of the kit completely clear of tools, steel, rags, or clutter.

- Consider a second smaller kit near the sink or eyewash station for quick eye-flush or hand-washing supplies.

- Protect the kit from grinding sparks, welding spatter, dust, and chemical splashes. A simple wall-mounted cabinet works best.

- Check the kit every month and restock immediately after use. An empty or expired first aid kit is almost as bad as not having one at all.

Note: Put the kit where it can actually save you, not where it looks pretty. The shop will not wait while you hunt for it.

Note: Anyone or everyone should immediately know exactly where the 1st Aid kit is in your shop.

"I've got it" from an apprentice usually means "hold my beer."

"

Section 5.2 – Burns & Heat Injuries

If there is one injury nearly every knifemaker will encounter, it is a burn. Heat is everywhere in the shop. It comes from glowing steel pulled from the forge, an oven cycling through tempering, or the torch used for a quick solder. Even tools you do not think of as hot can surprise you. A grinder working for ten seconds can warm steel enough to blister skin, and a freshly buffed blade can be hotter than you realize until it is too late. The real danger with burns is how easy it is to forget. Every maker has a moment where they have reached out for a piece of steel that looked cool but was not, or brushed against a forge wall without meaning to. One knifemaker tells of setting a blade down after quenching, then instinctively picking it back up bare-handed only to discover it was still more than hot enough to leave a mark. It is a simple mistake, and that is the point. Burns usually do not happen during big, dramatic accidents. They happen in the simple, everyday motions of shop work. What makes burns deceptively serious is that they do not always show their true depth immediately. A red mark can keep cooking tissue underneath the skin, and a small blister can become a painful infection if ignored. Worse, many makers shrug them off, slap on a band-aid, and go back to grinding. That tough-it-out mentality might feel like part of the trade, but it adds up over time. Repeated burns lead to scar tissue, reduced sensitivity, and long-term damage that cannot be undone. Take the proper time to treat an injury correctly.

Preparedness matters. A burn kit within arm's reach of the forge, non-stick dressings instead of shop rags, and the discipline to stop and treat a burn immediately are what separate a minor incident from a lasting injury. Burns are not just a nuisance. They are one of the most common and preventable injuries in a knife shop. Treating them with respect ensures you can keep working tomorrow instead of paying for shortcuts today.

Major Hazards Leading to Burns

- Hot Metal: Freshly forged or heat-treated steel looks the same as cold steel. Assume all steel is hot if the forge or oven is running.

- Quench Tanks: Oil can ignite, hot oil can splatter, and steam from water quench can scald.

- Torches & Open Flames: Oxy/acetylene and propane tools present direct flame and radiant heat risks.

- Grinding & Buffing: Friction can heat steel in seconds, and dropped pieces burn when they are caught instinctively.

- Finishing Rags: Oily rags can spontaneously combust, creating secondary fire hazards.

- Radiant Heat Exposure: Even standing close to a forge or oven can cause gradual burns or heat stress over time.

Visitors don't know your shop is trying to kill them.

First Aid Kit Additions for Burns

- Hydrogel Pads or Burn Gel: Cools tissue and provides immediate relief.

- Non-stick Sterile Dressings: Prevent sticking to raw skin and worsening damage.

- Cold Packs: For pain relief (never apply ice directly).

- Sterile Water or Saline: To flush and cool burns.

- Emergency Blanket: To manage shock in severe burn cases.

Safe Practices in Treating Burns

- Immediate Cooling: Run the burn under clean, cool (not cold) water for at least 10 minutes. This halts heat damage continuing beneath the skin.

- Do Not Apply: Oils, butter, ointments, or shop remedies. They trap heat.

- Proper Dressing: Cover with a sterile, non-stick dressing. Avoid adhesive gauze directly on the wound.

- Blisters: Do not pop them. They are natural barriers against infection.

- Seek Medical Help: For burns larger than a hand, burns that blister deeply, or burns involving face, joints, or airway.

- Working Alone: Have a clear plan for emergency contact. Burns can impair mobility and judgment quickly. Keep a phone or alarm accessible.

- Working with Others: Communicate. Label hot steel, announce "HOT" when moving material, and keep pathways clear to avoid accidental contact.

Note: Chemical burns and eye burns are covered in later subsections of Section 5.

Heat Exposure & Overheating

Burn injuries are not just from contact. Prolonged exposure to high shop temperatures can cause heat exhaustion or heat stroke.

- Heat Exhaustion Symptoms: Heavy sweating, weakness, dizziness, nausea.

- Heat Stroke Symptoms: Confusion, no sweating, rapid pulse, body temperature above 103 °F.

- First Aid: Move to a cooler area, loosen clothing, hydrate, and cool with damp cloths. Call emergency services if heat stroke is suspected.

Never trust a child who says "I just want to watch."

Practical Shop Notes

- Keep a small burn kit next to the forge or quench tank. Treatment delayed is treatment lost.

- Call out "HOT" when working with or around steel, tongs, or anvils if anyone else is in the shop.

- Keep drinking water or electrolytes on hand during forging sessions. Dehydration worsens heat stress.

- Burns may seem part of the trade, but repeat injuries build scar tissue that reduces sensitivity and grip over time. Treat every burn seriously.

Dogs don't understand "stay out of the sparks zone."

Section 5.3 – Cuts, Punctures, & Lacerations

If burns are one of the most common injuries in the shop, cuts are just as prevalent. In fact, most makers will experience more small cuts and punctures than they can count over the years. Sharp edges are everywhere. Knives in progress, chisels, saws, grinders, even freshly cut steel bar stock. A slip with a carving knife, a misjudged clamp on a drill press, or an unguarded buffing wheel can leave you bleeding before you realize what has happened. The tricky part is that most shop cuts do not feel dramatic. It is not always a screaming injury with blood everywhere. Sometimes it is a nick from a sharp burr, a metal splinter buried in your palm, or a scrape that does not seem worth cleaning up. That is where many makers make mistakes. They grab a paper towel, hold it for a minute, then get right back to grinding. Hours later the wound has reopened, it is full of grit, and infection has started to set in. What seemed like just a scratch now requires actual medical attention. One knifemaker tells of working a long night on a batch of blades, cutting his fingertip while clamping a tang. He wiped it off, wrapped it with electrical tape, and kept going. By the next day he could barely bend the finger. That is the real danger. Not the initial cut, but what happens when you ignore it.

Taking cuts seriously, no matter how small, is a discipline every craftsman must learn. First aid does not just stop the bleeding. It preserves your ability to keep working safely and comfortably in the long run.

Major Hazards Leading to Cuts & Punctures

- Sharp Tools & Blades: Knives, chisels, saws, and files all carry obvious risks.

- Grinding & Buffing: Abrasives leave edges razor-sharp long before the knife is finished.

- Broken Blades & Bits: Fragments from drills, saw blades, or snapped files are often jagged.

- Metal Splinters & Burrs: Steel filings and sharp bar ends pierce skin easily.

- Improper Workholding: Slipping workpieces or tools jumping out of clamps.

- Improper improvisation: Using a knife as a screwdriver, a file as a lever, or a sharp part as a handle.

Apprentices are how you learn what not to do… the hard way.

First Aid Kit Additions for Cuts

- Assorted Adhesive Bandages: Include fingertip, knuckle, large strip, and waterproof types.

- Sterile Gauze Pads & Rolls: For larger or deeper cuts.

- Antiseptic Wipes / Solutions: To clean wounds before dressing.

- Antibiotic Ointment: Helps prevent infection in minor cuts.

- Butterfly Closures or Steri-Strips: For drawing together small lacerations.

- Medical-Grade Superglue (Cyanoacrylate): Can be used to close small, clean cuts when bandages will not stay in place. Use only for non-contaminated wounds and never deep punctures.

- Tweezers: For removing splinters or debris.

- Medical Gloves: For treating wounds without contamination.

Safe Practices in Treating Cuts & Punctures

- Stop the Bleeding: Apply firm, direct pressure with gauze or a clean cloth. Hold pressure for several minutes. Do not keep peeking to see if it stopped.

- Clean Thoroughly: Flush with clean water or antiseptic solution. Removing dirt or metal filings is as important as closing the wound.

- Choose Closure Wisely:

  - Adhesive bandages work for very small cuts.

  - Butterfly closures or Steri-Strips are good for straight lacerations that want to stay open.

  - Medical-grade superglue (skin adhesive) can be used for small, clean cuts in areas where a bandage will not stay put. Never use shop glue and never on deep or dirty wounds.

- Apply & Protect the Bandage: Bandages only work if they stay clean, dry, and intact. Reinforce them with tape, finger cots, or waterproof coverings if you need to continue shop work.

- Watch for Infection: Redness, swelling, pus, or warmth around the wound means it needs medical attention.

- Seek Professional Care: For cuts longer than ½ inch, deep wounds that may involve tendons, or punctures from dirty metal or tools.

- Tetanus Reminder: Keep vaccinations up to date. Puncture wounds are a classic source.

- Do Not Hesitate to Call 911: If bleeding is severe, uncontrolled, or you are unsure what to do, call immediately. Operators are trained to walk you step by step through applying pressure, elevating the injury, or even using a tourniquet. Never second-guess the severity. It is better to call and not need it than to wait and risk permanent damage.

"Just one quick look" has ended more shop tours than you can count.

Note: Severe trauma, uncontrolled bleeding, or amputations are medical emergencies. Apply pressure, call 911, and follow the operator's instructions.

Practical Shop Notes

- Deburr steel stock before working. The first cut often happens before the knife is even shaped.

- Never reach blindly into scrap bins or under benches. Sharp surprises hide there.

- Clamp materials securely before drilling, filing, or grinding to prevent slips.

- Keep waterproof bandages on hand for fingertip cuts. They are among the most common shop injuries.

- Superglue is handy, but if you find yourself reaching for it every week, you are probably ignoring better prevention methods.

Your cat doesn't care about lockout/tagout.

Section 5.4 – Eye & Respiratory Emergencies

Your eyes and lungs are two of the most vulnerable and least replaceable parts of your body in the shop. Unlike hands or arms, they do not heal well from serious damage, and even small injuries can have lifelong effects. A deep cut may eventually scar over, but a scratched cornea or scarred lung tissue is damage you carry forever. That is why injuries to the eyes and lungs must be taken more seriously than almost any other hazard in the shop. The problem is that most of these dangers do not look like dangers at all. A faint haze of dust in the air does not seem threatening until it settles into your lungs day after day. A quick puff of smoke from soldering flux may burn your throat for an instant, but it is the repeated exposure that causes long-term irritation. A speck of metal bouncing off a grinder feels like nothing until you blink and realize it is embedded in your cornea. The worst part is that these hazards do not always hurt right away. Many makers can tell the same kind of story. They rub their eyes after grinding only to find out a tiny shard of steel is stuck where it does not belong, or they cough for weeks after breathing too much wood or resin dust. Others remember the first time they forgot their respirator while working with carbon fiber or G10. The scratchy throat and chest tightness are unforgettable. What all these stories have in common is how quickly a small exposure became a very big problem.

That is why prevention and immediate response are so critical. Eye protection and respirators are not optional accessories. They are the only barrier between you and injuries that do not heal easily, if at all. And when something does go wrong, knowing the right first aid steps, from flushing an eye properly to recognizing respiratory distress, can be the difference between a bad scare and a permanent injury.

Major Hazards Leading to Eye & Respiratory Injuries

- Flying Particles: Sparks, filings, scale, or broken abrasive fragments.

- Dust: Steel dust, wood dust, fiberglass, carbon fiber, bone, or exotic woods with natural toxins.

- Chemical Vapors: Acids, adhesives, solvents, and curing resins.

- Smoke & Fumes: From welding, brazing, burning rags, or overheated oils.

- High Air Pressure: Air tools and compressed air can blow debris directly into the eye.

- Welding & Bright Light: UV exposure causes flash burns (arc eye), a painful condition that feels like sand in the eye hours later.

Kids + grinders = YouTube videos you don't want to star in.

First Aid Kit Additions for Eye & Respiratory Emergencies

- Saline Eye Wash Bottles: For immediate flushing of debris.

- Eye Wash Station: If possible, a wall-mounted station with continuous flow.

- Eye Cups: For targeted rinsing.

- Sterile Eye Pads: To cover and protect injured eyes.

- N95 or P100 Respirators: For dusts and fibers.

- Cartridge Respirators: For chemical vapors.

- Spare Safety Glasses / Face Shields: To replace damaged or fogged PPE quickly.

Safe Practices in Treating Eye & Respiratory Injuries

Eye Injuries

- Flush immediately with clean water or saline for at least 15 minutes.

- Lean forward when flushing so contaminated water runs away, not into the other eye.

- Do not rub the eye. Rubbing can embed particles deeper.

- If the object does not flush out or is embedded, cover the eye with a sterile pad or cup and seek medical help.

- If one eye is injured, cover both. Eye movement is paired, so the injured one still moves when the other does.

Respiratory Irritation (Dust or Fumes)

- Move to fresh air immediately.

- Drink water to soothe the throat.

- Seek medical attention if coughing, wheezing, or shortness of breath persists.

Severe Respiratory Emergencies

- Call 911 immediately if breathing is impaired.

- Operators will guide you step by step in what to do until help arrives.

- If someone becomes unresponsive after fume inhalation, start CPR if you are trained.

Checklists exist because your memory is lying to you.

Chronic Exposure Risks

- Long-term dust inhalation (wood, bone, G10, carbon fiber) can cause fibrosis, asthma-like symptoms, or even cancer with certain materials.

- Chemical fume inhalation may cause delayed lung irritation (chemical pneumonitis). Symptoms like chest tightness or difficulty breathing hours later should never be ignored.

Asthma Attacks

- Makers with asthma should keep inhalers readily accessible.

- If medication does not help, or breathing worsens, call 911.

Note: Chemical burns to the eyes, or inhalation of toxic fumes, always require professional medical evaluation even if symptoms improve after first aid.

Practical Shop Notes

- Store a bottle of eye wash at every grinder, not just one for the whole shop.

- Keep extra respirator cartridges sealed in bags. Dirty or expired filters are useless.

- Do not use compressed air to clean dust off your clothes. It puts debris right into your eyes and lungs.

- Keep two sets of safety glasses: one clear, one tinted. If they scratch, replace them. Poor visibility increases risk.

- Always fit-test respirators. If you can smell fumes, your mask is not sealed.

- Know your materials. Carbon fiber, G10, and many exotic woods are harsher on lungs than plain steel dust.

- Dust collection systems are excellent, but sparks in a vacuum can ignite dust. Empty containers regularly and avoid mixing metal sparks with wood or resin dust.

That one safety rule you think is stupid? It's the one that will save you.

Section 5.5 – Chemical Burns & Exposures

In most knife and metalworking shops, chemicals do not look as threatening as a glowing forge or a screaming grinder. Bottles of epoxy, jars of acid, cleaners, oils, and solvents often sit quietly on a shelf until you need them. But do not be fooled by their stillness. Chemicals carry their own hazards, and those hazards are serious. Unlike cuts or burns from hot steel, chemical injuries do not always announce themselves right away. A splash of acid might sting immediately, but epoxy on bare skin can take hours to trigger a rash. Vapors from acetone or penetrating oil do not feel deadly at the moment, but after an evening in a poorly ventilated shop you might end up dizzy, nauseous, or with a headache that does not quit. Over time repeated exposures add up, sometimes leading to permanent allergies, skin conditions, or lung damage. What makes this worse is that many makers underestimate chemicals because they are so ordinary. Everyone has spilled a little superglue on their fingers, right? Or used acetone to clean brushes without gloves? The problem is not one-time exposure. It is building habits that dismiss the danger. That just a little epoxy becomes just a little rash, and eventually just a permanent skin allergy. The rag you left soaked in solvent does not just smell bad. It is a potential respiratory issue as well as a fire hazard.

The bottom line is knowing what you are working with is non-negotiable. Every chemical has its quirks, dangers, and proper handling methods. That is where Safety Data Sheets come in. They are the owner's manuals for every chemical in your shop, and if you do not know how to use them, you are working blind.

What Is an SDS?

A Safety Data Sheet (SDS) is a standardized document provided by manufacturers for every chemical product sold. It contains essential safety information, including:

- What the chemical is made of.
- How dangerous it is (flammability, health risks, reactivity).
- How to protect yourself while using it (PPE, ventilation, handling).
- What to do in case of spills, burns, or accidental exposure.
- How to store and dispose of it safely.

Think of it as the owner's manual for any chemical. If you do not know what the risks are, the SDS tells you.

The manual doesn't bite. Ignoring it does.

How to Find SDS Sheets

Most knifemakers do not realize that SDS sheets are not hidden away in secret databases. They are freely available online, and often provided directly by suppliers. Here is how to track them down:

1. Check the Label: Many products include the website of the manufacturer. Visit that site, search SDS or Safety Data Sheets, and enter the product name.

2. Google the Product Name + SDS: Type Epoxy Resin SDS or Loctite Super Glue SDS. Almost every time the official document will appear as a PDF on the manufacturer's site.

3. Ask the Seller: If you buy from a smaller shop or distributor, ask them directly for the SDS. By law (in most countries), sellers must provide it if requested.

4. Keep Your Own Copy: Download and print SDS sheets for every chemical you keep in your shop. Store them in a binder labeled SDS – Shop Safety. This way, if something goes wrong, you or someone helping you knows exactly what first aid steps apply to that specific chemical.

Major Hazards Leading to Chemical Burns & Exposures

- Acids & Bases: Ferric chloride, muriatic acid, and lye can cause severe skin and eye burns.

- Adhesives & Resins: Epoxy, CA glue, and accelerants can cause chemical burns, allergic reactions, or respiratory irritation.

- Solvents & Oils: Acetone, mineral spirits, penetrating oils, cutting oils, and waxes can strip skin oils, cause rashes, and give off harmful vapors.

- Cleaning Supplies: Bleach and ammonia are dangerous on their own, but mixing them creates toxic chlorine gas.

- Combustible Vapors: Many solvents ignite easily near sparks or open flames.

First Aid Kit Additions for Chemical Incidents

- Large Saline / Water Bottles: For immediate flushing of eyes and skin.

- pH-Neutralizing Solutions: Only if specifically advised by the SDS.

- Chemical-Resistant Gloves: Nitrile, neoprene, or rubber gloves chosen for compatibility with the chemical.

- Disposable Aprons or Sleeves: For mixing or etching.

- Emergency Shower Access: Even a garden hose is better than nothing if a splash covers you.

Repetition isn't nagging. It's how you stay alive.

Safe Practices in Treating Chemical Burns & Exposures

- Immediate Action: Flush with running water for 15 to 20 minutes. Remove contaminated clothing immediately.

- Do Not Neutralize: Unless the SDS directs otherwise, flushing with water is safest. Neutralizing reactions can cause heat and make burns worse.

- Eyes: Flush continuously with water or saline for at least 15 minutes. Cover with a sterile pad and seek medical help.

- Inhalation: Move to fresh air immediately. If dizziness or difficulty breathing continues, call 911.

- Skin Sensitizers: Epoxy and resins can cause lifelong skin allergies. Gloves and ventilation are mandatory.

- Disposal: Local hazardous waste rules apply. Never dump solvents, oils, or acids into drains or trash. Look up your city's hazardous waste drop-off.

Note: Always consult the Safety Data Sheet (SDS) for the chemical involved. First aid recommendations vary by material.

Note: Know what the SDS tells you about contact or spills before they happen. When you have a chemical in your eye is not the best time to attempt to read the SDS.

Practical Shop Notes

- Print or download SDS sheets for every chemical. Keep them in a binder marked SDS.

- Do not trust memory. If you are unsure how to handle a chemical, check its SDS before using it.

- Label all containers clearly. Mystery jars are accidents waiting to happen.

- Store acids and bases separately from solvents and combustibles.

- Rags soaked in oil or solvent should be kept in a sealed metal container to prevent both fire and skin contact.

- Ventilation is essential. If you can smell a solvent strongly, you are already inhaling too much of it

Safety isn't a one-time thing. It's a personality trait.

Section 5.6 – Fractures, Bruises & Soft-Tissue Injuries

Another set of injuries nearly every knifemaker will encounter is fractures, bruises, or soft-tissue damage. The shop is full of heavy steel, swinging hammers, anvils, grinders, belt sanders, and awkward reaches. A missed hammer strike, a dropped billet, a grinder that suddenly grabs, or even a simple slip on an oily floor can instantly turn a good forging day into weeks of recovery. Many makers have walked it off after a glancing hammer blow or steel clipping their foot, only to wake up the next morning with significant swelling that makes holding tongs or a file painful or impossible. Bruises can mask deeper damage.

Sprains can become chronic instability. An untreated fracture or dislocation can lead to months away from the forge or permanent loss of dexterity. What makes these injuries deceptively serious is how slowly some of them reveal their full impact. What feels like just a bad bruise today can develop into compartment syndrome or long-term scar tissue that reduces grip strength and fine motor control. The tough-it-out mentality common in knife making often delays proper treatment and turns minor incidents into lasting problems.

A well-stocked first aid kit and immediate use of the RICE protocol separate a short setback from a career-affecting injury. Proper immobilization when needed and the discipline to stop working make all the difference.

Major Hazards Leading to Fractures, Bruises & Soft-Tissue Injuries

- Dropped Objects: Heavy billets, hammers, anvils, or finished blades (especially feet, toes, and hands).

- Hammering & Forging: Missed strikes, rebound, flying scale, or chips.

- Machinery Issues: Grinders, belt sanders, or buffers grabbing material or kicking back.

- Slips, Trips & Falls: Oily floors, cluttered walkways, or fatigue.

- Improper Lifting / Carrying: Strains to back, shoulders, and knees when moving stock or equipment alone.

- Repetitive Stress: Long grinding, filing, or sanding sessions in poor posture.

- Pinching & Crushing: Vises, power hammers, presses, tongs, or shifting material.

The shop doesn't grade on a curve.

Prevention Strategies

- Wear steel-toed boots with good ankle support when forging or moving heavy stock.

- Keep your workspace clean and organized. Clear floors reduce trips and allow safe movement.

- Use proper body mechanics. Lift with your legs, keep your back straight, and get help with heavy pieces.

- Use appropriate tongs and tools instead of hands for holding hot or heavy material.

- Take micro-breaks during long grinding sessions and stretch regularly.

- Secure heavy items so they cannot shift or fall unexpectedly.

- Consider anti-fatigue mats if you stand for long periods.

First Aid Kit Additions for Fractures, Bruises & Soft-Tissue Injuries

- Instant Cold Packs or Reusable Ice Packs (always wrap before use).

- Elastic Compression Bandages (ACE wraps) in multiple sizes.

- SAM Splint or other moldable splinting material.

- Triangular bandages and slings for arm/shoulder support.

- Medical tape, padding, and gauze.

- Over-the-counter anti-inflammatory medication (Ibuprofen) and pain relief (follow dosage instructions).

- Sterile dressings for any associated open wounds.

Safe Practices in Treating Fractures, Bruises & Soft-Tissue Injuries

- Follow the RICE Protocol immediately:

  - Rest: Stop using the injured area completely.

  - Ice: Apply wrapped cold packs for 15 to 20 minutes every 1 to 2 hours (first 48 hours).

  - Compression: Use an elastic bandage to reduce swelling (not too tight, check for circulation).

  - Elevation: Keep the injured area raised above heart level when possible.

- Do not try to pop a dislocated joint back in place or force a deformed bone straight.

- For open fractures (bone through skin): Control bleeding with direct pressure and seek emergency care immediately.

- Monitor for signs of serious complications: increasing pain, numbness, tingling, coldness, or tightness (possible compartment syndrome).

If it feels sketchy, it probably is.

Distinguishing Between Injury Types

- Bruise (Contusion): Discoloration, swelling, tenderness from blunt force; usually no loss of function.

- Sprain: Ligament damage (overstretched or torn); swelling, bruising, pain with movement.

- Strain: Muscle or tendon damage; pain, stiffness, weakness.

- Fracture: Broken bone; sharp pain, swelling, deformity, inability to use the area, or grating sensation.

- Dislocation: Joint out of position; visible deformity, intense pain, locked joint.

Specific Common Knife Shop Injuries

Hand & Finger Injuries

- Very common from hammers, vises, and grinders. Immobilize carefully and seek medical evaluation quickly. Hands are critical for knife work.

Foot & Toe Injuries

- Dropped steel is a frequent cause. Steel-toed boots are highly recommended. Elevate and ice, but watch for fractures.

Back & Spine Strains

- Often caused by improper lifting or twisting while moving stock. Avoid heavy lifting alone. Use good posture and mechanical aids when possible.

Dislocations

- Usually occurs in fingers, shoulders, or wrists. Immobilize the joint in the position found and get professional help right away.

When to Seek Medical Help

- Obvious deformity or bone protruding through the skin.

- Inability to bear weight or use the limb/joint normally.

- Numbness, tingling, or loss of circulation below the injury.

- Severe swelling or pain that does not improve after 24 to 48 hours of RICE.

- Large, deep bruises, especially over joints.

- Any suspected fracture or dislocation.

Note: Severe trauma, suspected head/neck/spine injury, or heavy bleeding requires immediate emergency services (call 911).

Complacency is the real killer in the shop.

Recovery & Returning to Work

- Follow medical advice on immobilization and physical therapy.

- Gradually reintroduce movement and strength exercises once cleared.

- Modify your workflow temporarily (lighter stock, more assistance, shorter sessions).

- Build good habits to prevent re-injury. Many makers suffer the same injury multiple times.

You're not too good for safety rules. Nobody is.

Section 5.7 – Emergency Contacts & Planning

Emergencies are not polite. They do not wait until your shop is clean, your phone is charged, or your buddy is standing by with a first aid kit. They happen in the middle of projects, on late nights when you are tired, or when you have told yourself, I will only be out here for a few minutes. The truth is, many shops, especially small home or hobby shops, are completely unprepared for an accident. A missing phone charger, a cluttered exit, or not knowing the nearest hospital address can waste precious minutes. In a serious injury, those minutes are the difference between a close call and something far worse. Even professional shops can fall into the trap of assuming someone else will handle it. But in reality, the first line of response is always you, or whoever happens to be nearby. Without clear instructions, panic sets in fast. People do not know what number to call, where the first aid kit is, or how to explain where the shop is located to dispatch. That kind of confusion costs valuable time.

Planning ahead does not make you paranoid. It makes you smart. Posting phone numbers on the wall, keeping medical info in one place, and making sure everyone knows where the exits are may sound obvious, until the moment you need them and do not have them. Emergencies are chaotic by nature, but a clear plan brings order to the chaos and keeps injuries from becoming tragedies.

Major Considerations

Emergency Numbers (posted visibly)

- 911 (or local equivalent): The universal go-to, but always post it anyway.

- Fire Department (non-emergency line): For reporting hazards before they escalate.

- Nearest Hospital / Urgent Care: Include name, phone number, and address.

- Poison Control Hotline: Especially important for chemical exposures.

Personal Contacts

- Your spouse, partner, family, or trusted friend.

- Post more than one contact in case your first is not available.

- If you live rural, also list a nearby neighbor who could reach you faster than EMS.

Medical Information

- Allergies, chronic conditions, and medications should be written on a single sheet and kept in your first aid kit.

- Example: Allergic to penicillin, Diabetic, Asthma.

- Include blood type if known. It may save time in treatment.

The best safety device is the one between your ears.

Safe Practices in Emergency Planning

- Post It on the Wall: Numbers and addresses should be taped up, not buried in your phone. Your hands may be too messy, shaky, or injured to use a screen.

- Mark Your Address: Write your shop address in big, bold letters near the first aid kit. Even if you have lived there for years, panic can make you forget.

- Communication for Lone Workers: Let someone know when you will be in the shop and when you are expected out. Use check-in texts or alarms to remind you to respond periodically. Smartwatches or voice-activated assistants can call for help even if you cannot reach your phone.

- Location Awareness: Everyone who steps into your shop should know where the first aid kit, extinguishers, and exits are, even visitors.

- Emergency Roles: If multiple people are in the shop, assign roles: one calls 911, one administers aid, one meets responders at the entrance.

Advanced Planning

- GPS Coordinates: Especially useful for rural or hard-to-find properties. Post them with your address.

- Medical ID Apps: Many smartphones have a built-in Medical ID accessible even on a locked screen. Fill it out.

- Map Out Exits: Do not clutter exits with material. In a fire or chemical spill, every second matters.

- Practice Drills: Once in a while, walk through what you would do in a fire or severe injury. Muscle memory matters when adrenaline hits.

Practical Shop Notes

- Keep a spare phone charger or even a cheap backup phone in the shop if possible.

- If you live far from emergency services, consider keeping a trauma kit (tourniquet, chest seals, heavy gauze). It is better to have it and never use it.

- Update your emergency info every few months. Outdated contacts are useless.

The shop is always watching. And it has a terrible sense of humor.

Section 5.8 – Head Injuries & Concussions

Head injuries in the shop are one of the most underestimated dangers. Cuts, burns, or chemical splashes usually leave no doubt that something is wrong. They hurt, they bleed, or they make a mess. But head injuries are different. Sometimes they are dramatic, like a piece of stock falling from a rack onto your skull. Other times they are subtle: standing up too quickly into a shelf, slipping and hitting the floor, or taking a glancing blow from material thrown off a buffer. You might laugh it off, rub your head, and keep going, but what you do not see is the silent damage that can unfold hours later. Unlike a hand or an arm, your brain does not heal from injury in predictable ways. A small concussion can cause headaches, dizziness, and nausea that last for days. More severe impacts can alter memory, concentration, mood, and even personality. Some of these changes show up immediately, but others creep in quietly: a foggy mind, irritability, or delayed vomiting hours after the fact. Severe head trauma, when shrugged off, can lead to brain bleeds eventually leading to strokes. The danger is not just the injury itself, but the temptation to downplay it.

Many makers, especially those who pride themselves on toughness and self-reliance, try to shake it off. They will insist, I just got my bell rung or I will be fine. But concussions do not care how tough you are. The truth is that every head injury deserves respect, whether it came from slipping on sawdust or from a piece of bar stock bouncing off the floor into your face. This is why conversations with those around you are just as important as your own awareness. Your spouse, family, or shop partner may notice changes you do not: slurred speech, confusion, or unusual behavior. Neighbors or coworkers may be the ones who decide you need medical care when you would rather argue otherwise. Having those conversations ahead of time, before an accident, ensures that everyone knows what to look for, what to do, and how to override the stubborn maker who does not want help.

Head injuries are not something you can shrug off safely. They require planning, awareness, and sometimes persuasion, because protecting your brain is protecting everything else you do in life.

Major Hazards Leading to Head Injuries

- Falling Material: Unsecured bar stock, clamps, tools, or unfinished knives dropping from shelves.

- Overhead Hazards: Low beams, lights, or shelf edges in crowded shops.

- Slips & Trips: Falling onto concrete or against equipment.

- Machine Kickback: Buffers, grinders, or saws launching material with force.

- Fatigue & Distraction: Rushing or working while tired increases the risk of stupid accidents.

Gravity is undefeated. Don't test it.

Symptoms to Watch For

- Headache or pressure in the head.

- Dizziness, loss of balance, blurred or double vision.

- Nausea or vomiting.

- Confusion, memory lapses, or trouble concentrating.

- Slurred speech or difficulty forming words.

- Unusual drowsiness or passing out, even briefly.

- Pupils of unequal size or sudden changes in behavior/personality.

First Aid Response

- Stop Work Immediately: Do not shake it off and continue. Sit or lie down.

- Apply Ice: Use a cold pack or ice wrapped in cloth for swelling.

- Monitor Symptoms: Stay alert to changes over several hours. Many concussions worsen later.

- Call 911 Immediately If:

  - Loss of consciousness (even for a second).

  - Vomiting, confusion, or worsening headache.

  - Trouble waking the person or unusual drowsiness.

- Never Alone: A person with a head injury should not be left alone. Someone needs to monitor them.

- If Alone: Call 911 right away. The dispatcher can guide you through what to do until responders arrive.

Note: Unlike cuts or burns, you cannot tough out a head injury. Always treat it as serious.

Your tools are not aware… but sometimes they act like they are.

The People Around You Matter

- Talk to Your Spouse or Family: Make sure they know the signs of concussion and what to do if you come in saying you hit your head. Sometimes they will see changes (slurred speech, odd behavior) before you admit something is wrong.

- Tell Your Neighbors (if rural): If you live far from emergency services, having a trusted neighbor who knows what to do can be lifesaving. Share your shop address and a copy of emergency contacts.

- Inform Coworkers or Apprentices: If you work with others, make sure they know that a head injury is not a wait and see situation. Assign someone to monitor the injured person while another calls 911 if needed.

- Convincing the Tough Guy: Many makers resist help, insisting "I have a hard head". Here is the reality: brain injuries do not care how tough you are. Encourage persistence. Better safe than sorry. Remind them that EMS would rather be called and not needed than arrive too late.

Note: Sometimes it takes blunt conversations to convince an injured person they need help: You cannot grind steel if you cannot remember your own name.

Practical Shop Notes

- Wear a bump cap or hard hat if working under shelving or moving heavy stock overhead.

- Brightly mark low-clearance hazards with tape or paint.

- Store heavy material securely. Do not stack steel or wood where it can roll off.

- Keep floors clear of clutter to prevent slips and trips.

- Establish a simple rule with friends and family: if you hit your head and act off, they get to call 911 — no arguments.

"It's probably fine" is the last thing many makers ever thought.

Electrical Safety in the Knife Shop

When most makers think about safety in the knife shop, their minds jump to flying sparks, sharp edges, or heavy hammer blows. Electricity does not usually make the list until it does. Unlike grinders and forges, electricity is silent, invisible, and easy to take for granted. A cord plugged into the wall feels harmless enough, but behind that plug is the same force that powers welders, ovens, and entire buildings. Mismanaged, it can shock, burn, or start a fire faster than you can react. The challenge in small shops is that electrical safety often gets less attention than it deserves. Makers are more likely to buy a new belt grinder than to inspect the outlet it is plugged into. Extension cords from old Christmas lights get temporarily pressed into service. Power strips get overloaded, and dust builds up in outlets and switches. These shortcuts work fine until the day they do not. This section exists to keep electricity on your mind. It is not written to deter you away from using it. Without power, none of us would get very far. It is here to highlight how to use it wisely, maintain it properly, and prepare for the emergencies that sometimes come with it. The invisible hazards are real. Unlike fire or sharp edges, electrical dangers rarely give you a visual warning. A cord can look fine on the outside while heat builds inside. A grinder may run normally until the insulation in the switch finally fails. A missing ground prong does not make a spark every time. It just waits for the moment when it is needed and is not there. Even dust is a hidden player here. Fine metal particles do not just make a mess on your bench. They creep into outlets, switches, and tool housings. Add a little moisture and you have got a conductive paste that can short out circuits or give you a nasty jolt. That is why electrical safety is not only about cords and plugs. It is also about keeping your shop environment clean and dry. Electrical safety has two sides: prevention and response. Most of this section is about prevention, making sure cords are intact, outlets are grounded, tools are used properly, and lighting is adequate. But emergencies do happen. A shock can knock you off your feet, or a spark can turn into a small fire. When that happens, knowing the first steps, cutting power, using the right extinguisher, and calling 911 can mean the difference between a close call and a disaster. That is why we also focus on human factors: why people hesitate to call 911, why they downplay shocks, why they think a few wraps of tape on a cord is good enough. Good habits prevent most emergencies, but good training makes sure you handle the rest when they come. In a professional shop, electricians perform routine inspections. In a knife shop, you are the electrician whether you like it or not. That does not mean you need to memorize electrical code, but it does mean you should regularly check cords, plugs, and switches for heat or damage, verify outlets are grounded with a simple tester, blow grinder dust out of outlets and plugs with compressed air, keep your breaker box labeled and clear of clutter, and replace damaged cords or missing ground prongs immediately. These are quick habits, the kind you can build into your weekly cleanup or tool check, but they are the backbone of electrical safety.

Safety glasses: because eye patches are so last season.

Electricity is powerful, but it is also predictable. If you respect it, follow safe practices, and prepare for emergencies, it will work for you without becoming a constant hazard. The goal is not to make you afraid of plugging in your grinder. It is to make you aware of what is happening when you do, and to make sure your shop setup will not turn a small fault into a big problem. Think of it this way. Every grinder, forge, and light in your shop is powered by the same energy that runs through the high-voltage lines outside. That energy can build blades, or it can burn shops down. Which outcome you get comes down to how you manage it.

This section follows current OSHA 1910 Subpart S and NFPA 70 requirements for small shops.

The forge doesn't negotiate.

Section 6.1 – Wiring & Shop Electrical Setup

Electricity is the quiet danger in your shop. The forge roars, the grinder screams, the hammer rings, but electricity just hums in the background, powering it all. Because it is silent and invisible, it is easy to forget it can be every bit as dangerous as hot steel or spinning belts. When wiring fails or circuits are overloaded, you do not get sparks and drama right away. You get smoke in the walls, a warm outlet, or the faint smell of burning plastic. By the time you realize what is happening, you may already be standing in the middle of a fire incident. Most knife shops are not designed by electricians. They are set up in garages, barns, basements, and outbuildings, places that were never intended to power heat treat ovens, 2x72 grinders, dust collectors, air compressors, and bright shop lighting all at once. The wiring that was fine for a battery charger or a freezer can quickly become overwhelmed. That is how cords melt, breakers trip, and fires start behind drywall where you cannot see them. The problem is makers are resourceful, sometimes too resourceful. Instead of calling an electrician, it is tempting to run an extension cord across the floor, plug a power strip into another strip, or borrow the cord from the Christmas lights because it works. And it does, until the day it does not. The line between working and overheating is razor thin with electricity, and you often do not get a second chance. The good news is you do not need to be a licensed electrician to keep your shop safe. You just need to know a few key things: how to recognize overloaded circuits, what a safe extension cord looks like, why power strips are not all created equal, and how grinder dust can quietly build up inside outlets and switches until it causes a short. This section breaks down what to look for, what to avoid, and when to stop and call a professional, in plain language, without the jargon.

Think of this as your wiring survival guide. It is not about teaching you how to rewire your shop yourself, but about keeping you from burning it down.

Major Hazards in Shop Wiring

- Overloaded Circuits: Plugging too many high-draw tools into the same outlet or strip.

- Improvised Wiring: Extension cords used as permanent wiring or daisy chaining multiple power strips.

- Lack of Grounding: Old outlets or tools missing a ground prong increase shock and fire risk.

- Moisture Exposure: Outlets near sinks, water, or in humid shops without GFCI protection.

- Aging or Damaged Wiring: Cracked insulation, warm outlets, or buzzing breaker boxes.

- Dust Build-Up: Grinder dust settling inside outlets and switches, causing shorts or grounding failures.

That "quick fix" usually ends with a long recovery.

Extension Cords: What You Need to Know

- Gauge (Thickness): The lower the number, the heavier the cord.

  o   14 gauge: Light-duty (lamps, fans, Christmas lights).

  o   12 gauge: Medium-duty (drills, shop vacs, small grinders).

  o   10 gauge: Heavy-duty (welders, large grinders, dust collectors).

- Length Matters: The longer the cord, the more voltage drop. Use the shortest cord you can.

- Permanent Wiring: Extension cords are for temporary use only. If you leave one plugged in full-time, install a proper outlet.

Rule of Thumb: If it is thin and floppy like your holiday light cord, it is not safe for shop tools. Heavy-duty cords are thick, stiff, and labeled.

Power Strips: Safety Standards

- UL/ETL Listed: Only buy strips with certification. Cheap knock-offs often lack internal protection.

- 24/7 Use: Good strips can stay plugged in, but they are not for heavy shop tools. They are fine for chargers and lights, not grinders and ovens.

- Turn off power strips daily.

- Daisy-Chaining: Never plug a strip into another strip or into an extension cord. That is how cords melt.

- Load Balance: Use for small loads only. Multiple high-amp tools will overload even a quality strip.

Grinder Dust in Outlets & Switches

Metal dust conducts electricity, and over time it will creep into outlets, switches, and power strips:

- Short Circuits: Dust causes electricity to track across surfaces, leading to sparks or fires.

- Grounding Issues: Dust buildup can break down grounding, increasing shock risk.

- Prevention: Keep outlets and switches away from grinder stations. Use protective covers or sealed outlets if possible. Vacuum and clean outlets regularly (with power off).

Your shop is not a playground. It's a contact sport.

Signs You Have a Problem

- Outlets or plugs that feel hot.

- Breakers that trip often.

- Lights dimming when tools start.

- Buzzing, sizzling, or burning smells from outlets or cords.

- Visible sparks when plugging or unplugging.

Safe Practices

- Do not overload one circuit with multiple heavy tools.

- Use GFCI outlets in any area near quench tanks, water sources, or damp floors. This is required by OSHA and NFPA 70 for wet or damp locations.

- Label and clear access to breaker boxes.

- Do not run cords where they can be pinched, crushed, or tripped over.

- Unplug battery chargers when not in use. They can and do fail.

- Call an electrician if your shop wiring looks questionable.

First Response in Electrical Emergencies

- Electrical Fire: Use a Class C fire extinguisher. Never water.

- Shock Incident: Turn off the breaker if possible before touching the victim. If you cannot, use a dry wood or non-conductive object to push them free. Call 911 immediately. Shocks can cause delayed heart failure.

Practical Shop Notes

- Invest in a few 10 or 12 gauge cords for tools. They will stay cooler and safer.

- Mount outlets higher on the wall to reduce dust buildup.

- Do not face grinders directly at outlets. Sparks and dust will find a way in.

- Keep breaker access clear. Seconds matter in an emergency.

- A shop inspection by a licensed electrician can save you thousands in fire damage later.

Luck is not a safety plan.

Section 6.2 – Power Tools & Cords

Power tools are the backbone of a knife shop. Grinders, buffers, saws, drills, and sanders do the heavy lifting that no hand tool can. But all that performance relies on one humble but essential piece: the cord that brings them power. Unlike belts that wear thin or wheels that wobble, cords often fail quietly. Insulation cracks, prongs loosen, dust sneaks into switches, and the first sign of trouble might be a spark, a shock, or a tool that suddenly quits in your hands. Shops are harsh on cords. They are yanked, bent, stepped on, rolled over, and sprayed with grinder dust or quench water. Many cords fail right where they meet the tool. The strain breaks them down, the wires inside fatigue, and eventually the tool starts cutting out every time you move it. Some makers try to fix this with tape, zip ties, or splices, but these quick patches usually trade convenience for danger.

Cord safety is not glamorous, but it is critical. Taking a few minutes to inspect, replace, and properly route your cords can prevent shocks, fires, and sudden tool failures that put you at risk.

Major Hazards

- Frayed or Cracked Insulation: Exposed wires near the tool body or plug end.
- Loose or Damaged Plugs: Prongs bent, scorched, or no longer gripping securely.
- Broken Strain Relief: The reinforced collar where the cord enters the tool failing, causing internal wire breaks.
- Dust Infiltration: Fine grinder dust working its way into switches, plugs, or vents, leading to shorts.
- Improper Fixes: Wrapping tape around damaged spots instead of replacing the cord entirely.
- Trip Hazards: Long tool cords trailing across the shop floor.

Safe Practices

- Inspect Regularly: Look at cords and plugs before each session. Replace at the first sign of wear.
- Replace, Do Not Tape: Most tools have replacement cords available from the manufacturer. Do not patch what should be swapped.
- Protect the Strain Relief: Avoid sharp bends near the tool plug-in point. That is where most cords fail.
- Keep it Dry: Do not let cords hang near quench tanks or sit in puddles. Water and steel dust make a deadly mix.
- Unplug When Done: Prevents accidental starts and protects against overheating.

The shop always wins… unless you cheat with good habits.

Replacement Cords & Accessibility

Replacing cords is easier and safer than most makers realize.

- Availability: OEM replacement cords can be ordered directly from tool makers or through big-box hardware stores. Universal heavy-duty cords are also widely sold online.

- Fit & Rating: Choose cords rated for the tool's amperage and with proper strain relief. Avoid downgrading to thinner cords just because they are available.

- Ease of Replacement: Many power tools are designed for cord replacement with basic screwdrivers. For others, a service shop can install one cheaply.

- Cost vs. Risk: A $20 cord is a small price compared to a tool fried by a bad splice or a tool burning up causing a shop fire.

Signs of Cord or Plug Failure

- The tool cuts in and out when the cord moves.

- Cord feels warm in normal use.

- Melted, scorched, or bent prongs.

- Cracks or sticky spots in insulation.

- Burning smell from the plug or tool housing.

First Response If Something Goes Wrong

- Sparking Cord or Tool Plug: Unplug immediately (if safe) or cut power at the breaker.

- Shock Incident: Do not brush it off. Call 911 if there is chest pain, irregular heartbeat, or unconsciousness. Even small shocks can disrupt the heart.

- Electrical Fire: Use a Class C extinguisher. Never water.

Practical Shop Notes

- Always unplug tools by the plug, not the cord.

- Keep spare replacement cords for common shop tools. They are inexpensive and quick to swap.

- Coil cords loosely for storage. Avoid sharp kinks.

- Label cords by tool when spares are stored. Easy access means fewer excuses to keep using a bad one.

- Blow grinder dust out of switches and plugs regularly with compressed air.

- Train apprentices or helpers to report damaged cords instead of hiding them.

Hot steel has no respect for your weekend plans.

Lockout/Tagout

Before servicing any powered tool, unplug it and use a lockout/tagout device (or at minimum a tag that clearly states "Do Not Energize") so no one can accidentally plug it back in. This meets OSHA 1910.147 requirements and prevents unexpected startup.

The buffer is silent until it launches your blade like a missile.

Section 6.3 – Grounding & Bonding

Grounding and bonding are two of the most misunderstood parts of electrical safety in small shops. To many makers they feel like technical jargon reserved for electricians. But in reality grounding is what keeps electricity from turning your shop into a shock hazard, and bonding ensures that all your equipment is safely connected to the same electrical reference point. Without them even a minor wiring issue could turn the frame of your grinder, drill press, or dust collector into a live conductor waiting for your touch. For knife shops grounding is especially critical because we work around metal dust, moisture, and high-powered equipment. A frayed wire in a grinder, a poorly wired extension, or even static electricity from dust collection can all become serious hazards if grounding is not in place.

The good news is you do not need to be an electrician to understand every detail of grounding. Knowing what grounding is, how to check it, and how to prevent common failures can go a long way toward protecting yourself.

Major Hazards

- Shock Hazards from Ungrounded Tools: If a wire comes loose inside a tool and the case is not grounded, touching it could complete the circuit through your body.

- Static Electricity Build-Up: Dust collection systems, especially with fine metal or wood dust, can create static charges strong enough to arc or ignite dust.

- Improper Bonding: Tools and dust collection pipes not bonded together may carry different charges, increasing the risk of sparks.

- Broken Ground Prongs: Many tools get their ground prong snapped off to fit an old outlet. This removes your main safety feature.

Safe Practices

- Never Remove Ground Prongs: If your tool came with a 3-prong plug, it needs all three. Replace the outlet, do not "fix" the tool.

- Check Your Outlets: Use an inexpensive outlet tester sold at any hardware store to verify that outlets are properly grounded.

- Bonding Dust Collection: Run a ground wire along metal dust collection ducting and bond all parts together. For plastic hose use an external copper wire wrap to bleed static charges away.

- Inspect Cords & Plugs: Replace any tool cord missing a ground prong. A two-prong "fix" is not a safe solution.

- Ground Equipment: Ensure large stationary tools grinders, drill presses, heat treat ovens are plugged into grounded outlets.

Sparks don't ask permission.

Signs of Grounding Problems

- Tingling or buzzing sensation when touching a tool metal body.

- Sparks when connecting or disconnecting dust hoses.

- Frequent static shocks when working around grinders or dust collection systems.

- Breakers tripping without clear cause.

First Response in an Emergency

- Shock Incident: Disconnect power immediately at the breaker if possible.

- If the victim is still in contact with live equipment: Do not touch the victim directly. Use a non-conductive object to attempt to separate them from the equipment. Call 911.

- Dust Fire or Spark Ignition: Shut down dust collection and use a Class C fire extinguisher. Do not try to smother an electrical dust fire with water.

Practical Shop Notes

- Buy an inexpensive outlet tester and check every outlet in your shop. It is a cheap peace of mind.

- Run a dedicated ground wire to large stationary tools if your shop wiring is questionable.

- Do not ignore little zaps or static shocks. They are your warning sign, not a quirk of the tool.

- For dust collection keep hoses short, bond ducting, and ground your system. A static spark in a dust cloud is more dangerous than most makers realize.

- If in doubt about shop grounding, call an electrician for an inspection. It is one of the fastest ways to improve shop safety.

Your respirator is not optional. It's your lungs' only fan club.

Section 6.4 – Electrical Fires & Shock Response

Electrical emergencies do not give you time to think. A cord that smolders or a shock that locks your muscles can turn a normal day in the shop into a crisis in seconds. Unlike mechanical injuries, where you can usually see and feel danger coming, electricity is silent until it strikes. Then you have only moments to act.

That is why this section is less about prevention (covered earlier) and more about what to do the instant something goes wrong. Fires and shocks require calm, clear action. Hesitation can make the difference between a close call and a tragedy.

First Response: Electrical Fires

- Cut the Power First: If you can, kill the breaker that feeds the outlet or tool.

- Use the Right Extinguisher: Aim a Class C (or ABC multipurpose) extinguisher at the base of flames. Never use water.

- Call 911: If the fire does not go out immediately, evacuate and call. Fire spreads shockingly fast in dust-filled spaces.

- Follow Dispatcher Prompts: Emergency operators can guide you on whether to fight or evacuate, depending on the situation.

First Response: Electrical Shocks

- Break Contact Safely: If the victim is still in contact with electricity, shut off the breaker or unplug. If you cannot, use a dry wooden broom handle or other non-conductive tool to separate them. Never grab them directly.

- Cut Power: Flip the breaker or unplug if safe to do so.

- Call 911 Immediately: Even if the victim seems okay. Shocks can cause delayed heart or breathing problems.

- Follow Dispatcher Prompts: 911 operators can talk you through CPR, AED use, or stabilizing the victim until EMS arrives.

- CPR / AED: If the victim is unresponsive and not breathing, begin CPR immediately. Use an AED if available.

- **Arc-Flash Burns**: Even a small arc can cause severe burns. Treat any electrical burn as serious and seek immediate medical care. Wear flame-resistant clothing when working near live panels if you are qualified.

That one loose wire is auditioning for "how to start a fire."

Why People Hesitate and Why You Should Not

Makers are stubborn by nature. That stubbornness saves us money and gets knives finished, but it can also get us killed when something goes wrong. Here is why people freeze or downplay an emergency and why you must not.

- **Minimizing the injury** Makers often downplay a shock or a little smoke. A small zap today can stop your heart tomorrow. A little smoke can turn your shop into a total loss in under five minutes. Treat every incident like it is serious. The shop will not give you a second chance to change your mind.

- **Fear of overreacting** Some makers hesitate to call 911 because they do not want to waste the operator's time or look foolish. Do not hesitate. The operator's only job is to help you. It is always better to overreact and be wrong than to underreact and be dead. Call early. Let them tell you it is nothing. You will still be alive to feel embarrassed.

- **Adrenaline freeze** In a real crisis your brain can stall completely. You stand there thinking "this is not happening" while valuable seconds disappear. That is exactly why you rehearse these steps and teach everyone in your household or shop what to do. Muscle memory beats panic every single time.

- **Stubborn "tough guy" mentality** Many makers think calling for help makes them look weak. The shop does not care how tough you are. It only cares how fast you bleed or how hot the fire gets. Pride has put more makers in the hospital than a chock or cut ever has. Swallow it, call for help, and get back to making knives.

- **Worry about cost or downtime** Some makers hesitate because they do not want the ambulance bill or the lost shop time. The real cost is far higher if you wait. A few hours of downtime is nothing compared to months of recovery or a closed shop because you are gone. The bill you pay today is always cheaper than the one the hospital sends later.

Note: Immediate action is the difference between getting back to the bench in a day or never picking up a file again. Hesitation does not make you look strong. It makes you look foolish.

The vise doesn't care if you're in a hurry.

Section 6.5 – Lighting & Emergency Power

Lighting in a knife shop is one of those things that many makers do not think about until they realize something is wrong. You might start with whatever bulbs the garage or basement came with, add a clamp light or two, and tell yourself it is good enough. But poor lighting does not just make your shop feel dark. It directly affects your safety and the quality of your work. Imagine trying to line up a drill bit with a tang hole while your own shadow blocks your view. Or imagine trying to grind bevels straight when one side of the platen is brightly lit and the other side is buried in dimness. Shadows, blind spots, and flicker do not just make it harder to work. They lead to crooked grinds, missed cracks in steel, and sometimes accidents that could have been avoided with proper lighting. Good lighting is as much a safety measure as your respirator or eye protection. Emergency power is added in another layer. Knife shops often operate in outbuildings, garages, or rural spaces where power is not always reliable. A sudden blackout when you are holding a piece of glowing steel or running a grinder at full speed can turn into chaos instantly. In total darkness it is not just that you cannot see the workpiece. You cannot see the hazards around you either. Quench tanks, sharp blades, hot forges, and moving belts do not suddenly stop being dangerous just because the lights went out.

That is why planning for both good everyday lighting and emergency lighting is so critical. Everyday lighting keeps you working safely and comfortably, while emergency lighting and power keep you from being caught blind in the middle of a dangerous process. You do not need to spend a fortune to get it right, but you do need a plan. A few smart choices can make the difference between calmly shutting down your shop in an outage or stumbling through a minefield of sharp and hot hazards in total darkness.

Major Hazards

- Dim or Inconsistent Lighting: Hidden edges, poor blade alignment, and overlooked cracks in material.

- Glare & Shadow: Badly positioned lights create optical illusions that can mislead your eyes.

- Power Outages During Work: Losing visibility mid-grind or mid-forge increases injury risk.

- Improvised Lamps: Cheap clip lights, unshielded bulbs, or extension-light setups often create fire hazards.

- Return of Power Surges: When electricity comes back on, a surge can fry your tools if they were not unplugged.

Wood chips are not confetti.

Safe Practices

Everyday Lighting

- General Illumination: Use overhead LED fixtures for bright, even coverage. LEDs run cooler, last longer, and resist vibration better than fluorescent or incandescent bulbs.

- Task Lighting: Equip grinders, drill presses, and benches with adjustable task lights. Position them to eliminate shadows, not just add more light.

- Color Temperature: Use daylight-rated bulbs (around 5000 K) to reduce eye strain and show true colors in steel and wood.

Emergency Lighting

- Why It Matters: Think of emergency lighting as insurance. A blackout in the middle of grinding or forging can leave you one misstep away from injury. Compared to the cost of medical care or lost shop time, even modest investments in backup lighting pay for themselves many times over.

- Cost vs. Injury: The price of a backup light is trivial compared to stitches, burns, or the damage from fumbling in total darkness. A single backup fixture or headlamp costs less than many consumables and does far more to protect you.

- Cost-Conscious Options: Rechargeable flashlights and headlamps. Rechargeable LED work lights. Battery-powered emergency fixtures. Solar yard lights (repurposed). Glow-in-the-dark tape.

Emergency Power

- UPS Units: Small uninterruptible power supplies can keep lights, ventilation fans, or even your computer on long enough for a safe shutdown.

- Generators: Portable generators are useful for extended outages but must be run outside only to avoid carbon monoxide poisoning. Generators must always be run outside only. Never operate one inside or near open doors/windows. Carbon monoxide is invisible and can kill quickly.

- Battery Backup: Rechargeable LED lanterns and floodlights should be tested regularly. A dead light is as useless as none at all.

The grinder wheel is one crack away from becoming shrapnel.

First Response in a Blackout

1. Hands Off Immediately: If you lose light, let go of machines at once. Do not try to finish a grind or cut blind.

2. Secure Hot Work: Place hot steel flat on the anvil or in a heat-safe tray so you can move safely.

3. Switch to Emergency Lighting: Use mounted emergency fixtures or grab a flashlight or headlamp.

4. Shut Down Equipment: Once safe light is restored, unplug or switch off machines until the power is stable again. Surges can damage motors and controls.

Practical Shop Notes

- Think of lighting as PPE for your eyes. You cannot protect what you cannot see.
- Place at least two emergency lights so no part of the shop is pitch black.
- Store flashlights and headlamps in clearly labeled, reachable spots.
- Add reflective or glow tape on breaker boxes and exit doors.
- Test emergency power setups monthly. Dead batteries always seem to show up when you need them most.
- If you use a generator, practice setting it up in daylight before you need it in a blackout.

"I'll clean it later" is how fires get started.

Personal Considerations

When most people think about shop safety, they picture goggles, gloves, or fire extinguishers. They imagine sparks flying off grinders and machines whirling. But one of the most overlooked aspects of safety is not hanging on the wall or plugged into the outlet. It is you. The person who walks into the shop each day is the most critical piece of the safety puzzle. This section focuses on personal considerations; the mindset, habits, and choices that keep you steady long before a tool is switched on. Machines do not care about your mood, your posture, or how much sleep you got last night, but those things directly affect how you interact with your tools. A tired or distracted maker is more likely to skip precautions. A maker pushing through pain may ignore warning signs of injury. A maker convinced they do not need help might push themselves into situations that are both unnecessary and dangerous. The truth is simple. Your health, your focus, and your humility shape your shop environment as much as your layout or your equipment. Safety gear protects you from sparks, dust, or cuts, but only if you wear it. Fire extinguishers save shops, but only if you grab them in time. Preparation, discipline, and awareness are the habits that make all those physical safety measures useful. And those habits do not happen by accident. They come from the way you approach the work. A maker who enters the shop with a clear head, rested body, and patient attitude is already safer than one who staggers in exhaustion or anger. Accidents are rarely just about the tool. They are about the person running it. A belt grinder is dangerous no matter who uses it, but it is especially dangerous for someone rushing, distracted, or arrogant. This section reminds us that safety starts with the person, not the equipment. Machines may cut, burn, and break, but it is the human decisions around those machines that determine the outcome. Physical conditions play a massive role in how you interact with your tools. The strongest vise grip in the world will not matter if your hands are too sore to hold steady. Hours of repetitive grinding can inflame tendons. Standing hunched at a bench can wreck your back. In the long-term, these injuries can end a maker's journey altogether. On the other side, mental health and mindset are just as critical. A shop can be a place of focus and relaxation, or it can become a pressure cooker where stress builds and mistakes multiply. It is easy to underestimate the toll of fatigue, anxiety, or the stubborn belief that tough guys do not need help. That mentality does not protect anyone. It isolates and endangers. Together the physical and mental sides of safety form a loop. A tired body wears out your focus. A distracted mind forgets to move safely. Respecting both is how you break the cycle and stay steady at the workbench. How you show up physically also shapes your safety. Long hair, big beards, loose sleeves, and dangling jewelry may look fine outside the shop, but inside they are just another hazard. Machines do not need much to pull you in. The same goes for footwear and clothing. If you would not wear flip-flops on a construction site, do not wear them near a forge or grinder. It may sound obvious, but day-to-day it is easy to forget. Many accidents are not about doing something crazy. They are about something simple, like forgetting to roll up a sleeve or thinking I will just grab this real quick. Grooming and appearance may not feel like safety topics, but they are part of the bigger picture of preparation.

Your shop apron is not a cape.

For many knifemakers solitude is part of the appeal. The quiet rhythm of the forge, the sound of a grinder, the chance to focus, these are often best enjoyed alone. But working alone means you are also your own safety net. A dangerous cut that would be no big deal with someone nearby can spiral quickly when you are by yourself. A heavy machine that tips, fumes that overwhelm, or simply forgetting to check in with someone can turn isolation into danger. That is why preparation is key. Keeping a phone within reach, letting someone know your schedule, and avoiding the riskiest tasks when completely alone, are small steps with huge payoffs. You do not have to give up solo shop time. You just need to approach it differently. Confidence is required to make knives. Without confidence every hammer strike and grinder pass feels shaky. But confidence is not the same as arrogance. Confidence is earned through practice and preparation. Arrogance is assuming the rules do not apply to you. One keeps you safe. The other puts you in harm's way. A strong safety mindset is a balance. It is the humility to slow down and double-check, the openness to ask questions, and the wisdom to admit when you need help. It is reminding yourself that the shop does not forgive complacency, and that "I will be fine" is not a safety plan. The best makers are not the ones who act as if they are indestructible. They are the ones who stay curious, humble, and cautious enough to keep working year after year.

Section 7 ties all these threads into a single truth. You are the most important tool in your shop. Machines, materials, and techniques matter, but they all rely on you showing up focused, prepared, and humble. Safety is not just about PPE or fire extinguishers. It is about how you treat your body, how you manage your mind, how you present yourself physically, how you prepare when working alone, and how you balance confidence with humility. When these personal considerations come first, everything else in the shop flows smoother. Work becomes steadier. Injuries are fewer. Projects finish with more satisfaction and less regret. This is not a section to skip. It is the foundation for everything else that follows. Knifemaking is a craft that demands more than sharp steel and steady hands. It demands a sharp mind, a strong body, and a clear understanding of how you show up to the shop every single day. Your mental state, physical condition, grooming habits, decision to work alone, and overall safety mindset are not side issues. They are the foundation that either protects you or quietly sets you up for failure.

This section covers the human side of shop safety: mental health and focus, physical fitness and ergonomics, grooming and personal appearance, the unique risks of working alone, and the critical balance between confidence and caution. These personal factors align with OSHA guidelines on workplace fatigue, lone-worker safety, and the human-performance side of hazard control. Ignoring any of them can turn a routine shop day into a trip to the emergency room or worse.

The quench tank is not a swimming pool.

Section 7.1 – Mental Health & Focus

Knifemaking is often seen as a craft of grit and solitude. Many makers are proud of working alone, pushing through frustration, and figuring things out with nothing but stubbornness and sweat. There is honor in persistence, but there is danger in pride. The tough guy mindset of "I do not need help" and "I will just push through" may seem harmless, but in the shop it can be deadly. Think about it. You are grinding late at night, already tired from a long day. Your head is in another place focusing on bills, family arguments, or just sheer exhaustion. The belt begins to wander on the grinder, but you are so locked into finishing this one last pass that you do not stop to fix it. In the blink of an eye the blade snags, the grinder bites, and you are left staring at a gouge in the steel or worse, a gouge in your forehead. That accident was not caused by ignorance. It was caused by distraction, pride, and fatigue. The shop does not care if you are having a bad day. It does not care if you are anxious, depressed, or furious. Machines do not slow down just because your mind is racing. Steel does not cool down just because you are thinking about something else. The forge, the grinder, the saw, they all demand your full focus. If you do not have it, they will take advantage of the smallest slip. Many makers quietly wrestle with stress, burnout, or even depression. Some try to bury those feelings by working harder, as if more time in the shop will solve what is going on inside. Others wear toughness like armor, refusing to admit that they are struggling. But toughness does not mean silence. Real toughness is being honest enough to say I am not okay right now and I need help. And the harder truth is some makers fight battles darker than stress or distraction. Suicidal thoughts are not rare, though they are rarely spoken about in shop culture. That silence can be deadly. If you are carrying that weight, walking into the shop alone with sharp steel and heavy machines is not the answer. It is not a weakness to step back and call someone, it is strength. It may be the most important safety step you will ever take.

Mental health is not separate from shop safety. It is not extra. It is as essential as goggles, respirators, and fire extinguishers. A sharp, focused mind is your first layer of protection, and caring for that mind through rest, support, family, faith, or community is what keeps you alive, uninjured, and able to enjoy the craft tomorrow.

Major Hazards

- Distraction: Worry, stress, or racing thoughts make it harder to notice details that prevent accidents.

- Tough Guy Mentality: Refusing to slow down, ask questions, or admit fatigue.

- Isolation: Working alone without support increases both shop risk and mental strain.

- Family Disconnect: Ignoring the role of spouses and kids in your balance and well-being.

- Neglected Outlets: Without positive ways to release stress, negativity builds until mistakes follow.

- Suicidal Thoughts: The most dangerous hazard of all. One that must be addressed openly and seriously.

That magnetic chuck is only as strong as the last time you cleaned it.

Safe Practices for Mental Health

Asking for Help

- In the Shop: If you do not understand a process, ask. Heat treating, forging, and even basic grinding each have learning curves, and forcing your way through in silence is how mistakes happen.

- On Projects: Do not waste time fighting the same error over and over. A short conversation with a fellow maker can save hours of frustration and reduce risk.

- With Heavy Lifts or Setup: Get a hand when moving anvils, billets, or machines. Injuries from pride last longer than the five minutes it would have taken to ask.

- At Home: Share your stresses and frustrations. Spouses and kids cannot help if you keep it all locked away.

Family & Relationships

- Spouses and Partners: They are not just bystanders. They are part of your safety system. Involving them in your world, even by explaining what you are working on, can strengthen both your mental state and your shop safety.

- Kids: Seeing you work safely sets an example. They are also a living reminder of why coming home in one piece matters more than rushing a project.

- Support Network: Let family and friends be the balance that helps you step out of the shop when you are mentally spent.

Positive Mindset

- Patience Over Pride: Slowing down is not weakness. It is being in full control.

- Celebrate Progress: Even imperfect knives mean lessons learned.

- Shift the Lens: See setbacks as part of growth instead of proof of failure.

- Focus on the right things: acknowledge what was done right. Do not allow what went wrong to consume you.

Healthy Outlets

- Religion and Faith: For many, prayer, worship, or meditation provide grounding and peace.

- Gym and Fitness: Exercise clears stress, boosts focus, and strengthens the body you rely on in the shop.

- Groups and Community: Whether it is a blacksmith meet-up, maker forum, or support group, connection builds resilience.

- Nature: Step away from the shop for a few moments to find peace in nature.

The lathe doesn't care about your ego.

If You Are Struggling with Suicidal Thoughts

- You are not alone. Many makers and craftsmen have faced this darkness.

- Talk to someone. Family, friends, fellow makers, or a professional. Speaking the words breaks the hold.

- Emergency Help: In the U.S.

dial 988 for the Suicide and Crisis Lifeline (24/7)

Outside the U.S., find your local hotline.

Shop Rule: Never step into the shop when you are in a suicidal mindset. Power tools and hot steel are not a cure. Walk away, get help, make the call. Let the work wait.

Practical Shop Notes

- Keep a small trusted circle of knifemaking friends you can call when your head is not right. Isolation makes every problem worse.

- Balance shop time with real life. Family, friends, and time completely away from the tasks are not luxuries. They keep you mentally sharp and physically safe in the shop.

- Place visible reminders in your shop of why you make knives. A photo of your kids, your spouse, or even your dog. A meaningful verse or quote. Something that brings you back when frustration starts building.

- Check in with yourself honestly before you turn on any machine. Ask: Am I clear-headed enough to do this safely today? If the answer is no or even maybe, walk away. The project will wait.

- Build regular positive outlets outside the shop to manage stress. Exercise, faith, hobbies, or time with people who have nothing to do with knives. A clear mind is a safe mind.

- Learn to recognize when mental fatigue or frustration is creeping in. Step away before that feeling turns into a mistake with a grinder, hot steel, or a sharp edge.

- Have a firm bad-day rule. If your mind is not right, shut the lights off and leave the shop. Coming back the next day with a clear head is always smarter than forcing it today.

- Move your body regularly. Physical fatigue quickly becomes mental fatigue. A strong, rested body supports a focused mind in the shop.

- Know when it is time to ask for real help. If the weight stays heavy for too long, talk to someone who is trained to carry it. Strength is knowing when you need support.

Dust collection is not a suggestion.

Practical Tips for Building Real Shop Confidence

- Keep your shop clean and organized every single day. A professional workspace gives you a professional mindset.

- Master one machine or process completely before moving to the next. Real confidence comes from competence, not from rushing.

- Use checklists and routines religiously. Checking off boxes is not weakness, it is how professionals stay sharp.

- Display your finished knives where you can see them while you work. Every time you look up and see good work, your brain remembers you are capable.

- Wear your PPE properly and consistently. When you look like a pro, you start thinking and acting like one.

- Celebrate small wins out loud. Finished a perfect bevel? Say it. Ground a clean spine? Tell someone about it. Positive reinforcement wires your brain for safety and success.

- Know your limits and respect them. The most confident makers are the ones who say "not today" when their head or body is not right.

- Teach someone else what you know. Nothing builds confidence faster than realizing you have knowledge worth sharing.

When you walk into your shop and feel like you belong there, the shop stops feeling like an enemy and starts feeling like a partner. That is the difference between surviving the craft and truly owning it.

Your phone can wait. The shop won't.

Section 7.2 – Physical Condition & Fitness

Your body is the most important and most expensive tool in the shop. You can buy new grinders, swap out belts, or replace a broken anvil, but you do not get to order a replacement back or wrist off of Amazon Prime. Once your body is injured, recovery is slow, expensive, and often incomplete. Knifemaking puts stress on the body in ways that sneak up on you. Hours of repetitive grinding, endless filing, swinging hammers, and standing in one position all add up. At first it is just soreness, then it becomes stiffness. If ignored long enough, it can become a permanent injury. Conditions like carpal tunnel, tennis elbow, arthritis, and chronic back pain do not often announce themselves with a single dramatic accident. They build quietly over time, one bad posture or one overextended grip at a time. By the time you realize how bad it is, it may be too late to undo. This is why paying attention to your physical condition, strength, flexibility, endurance, and rest, is every bit as much about safety as eye protection or respirators. A fit, rested maker has quicker reactions, steadier hands, and sharper focus. A fatigued, sore, or injured maker is more likely to slip, drop, or misjudge.

Major Hazards

- Repetitive Motions: Hours of grinding or sanding without breaks lead to wrist, elbow, and shoulder strain.

- Improper Grip and Force: Forcing tools instead of letting them cut leads to tendonitis, arthritis, and nerve compression.

- Poor Posture: Leaning into the grinder, hunching over a bench, or twisting awkwardly leads to neck and back problems.

- Fatigue and Weakness: Reduced reaction time and higher likelihood of mishandling sharp or hot tools.

- Ignoring Pain: Treating aches as normal leads to chronic, sometimes irreversible injury.

Safe Practices and Prevention

Stretching and Mobility

- Wrists and Hands: Extend arms and gently pull fingers back to stretch forearm flexors. Rotate wrists clockwise and counterclockwise to keep joints loose. Shake out hands regularly during grinding sessions.

- Elbows and Shoulders: Cross body arm stretches to loosen shoulders. Light forearm flex and extension stretches help prevent tennis elbow.

- Back and Core: Gentle twists, hip openers, and standing bends before and after long shop sessions. Engage your core muscles when lifting heavy objects to protect your spine.

- Legs and Knees: Use calf raises and mini squats every hour to keep circulation moving. Wear supportive boots and consider anti fatigue mats.

Safety is the only thing that lets you keep making knives tomorrow.

Carpal Tunnel Syndrome

- Keep wrists in a neutral, straight position. Avoid bending up or down when filing or grinding.

- Do not use death grips on tools. Hold them firmly but let abrasives do the cutting.

- Break up long grinding or sanding sessions with lighter tasks.

Tennis Elbow (Lateral Epicondylitis)

- Caused by repetitive twisting and gripping motions.

- Avoid excessive torque. Do not over tighten clamps or twist tools aggressively.

- Switch hands when possible to balance strain.

Arthritis and Long Term Wear

- Warm up joints before working in a cold shop. Cold tendons are stiffer and more vulnerable.

- Hydrate. Dehydration makes joints and cartilage more prone to irritation.

- Use ergonomic handles or cushioned grips on tools where possible.

Lifting and Overexertion

- Bend at the knees, keep your back straight, and hold the load close.

- Never try to move large anvils, steel bars, or machines alone.

- Use dollies, carts, or a second person instead of toughing it out.

Practical Shop Notes

- Rotate tasks. Do not spend six hours grinding without switching to fitting or finishing work if possible.

- Adjust work surfaces to match your height. Grinders, benches, and anvils should fit you, not the other way around.

- Invest in anti fatigue mats for long standing tasks.

- Keep shop shoes supportive. Cheap sneakers will not protect your joints over the long haul.

- Treat shop time like physical labor. Fuel properly, hydrate, stretch, and rest afterward.

The shop is patient. It will wait for you to get lazy.

Section 7.3 – Grooming & Personal Appearance

How you present yourself in the shop is not about fashion. It is about safety. Machines do not care if you look sharp or scruffy, but they do care about what they can grab. Hair, beards, loose sleeves, dangling jewelry, and poor footwear are all invitations for accidents. And once something gets caught, machines do not let go. The way you dress, trim, and prepare yourself before stepping into the shop is as important as putting on safety glasses. It is not about being neat. It is about being smart. Small decisions such as tying back your hair, tucking in a shirt, or leaving jewelry on the bench can mean the difference between a smooth shop session and a serious injury.

Major Hazards

- Loose Clothing: Baggy shirts, hoodie strings, or rolled sleeves slipping down can snag in grinders, drills, or buffers.

- Long Hair and Beards: Untied hair or free hanging beards are prime targets for rotating tools.

- Jewelry: Rings, watches, and necklaces can snag, conduct electricity, or cause crushing injuries.

- Improper Footwear: Sneakers, sandals, or worn out boots offer little protection against dropped blades, hot steel, or slick floors.

- Dust and Hygiene: Fine dust clings to hair, beards, and clothing, causing irritation and exposing your family when carried into the house.

Safe Practices

Hair and Beards

- Tie back long hair securely. Do not just tuck it in your collar.

- For long beards, braid and/or tie them back when working in the shop.

- If your beard is long enough to reach the workpiece, it is long enough to be a hazard.

Clothing

- Stick to fitted cotton or natural fiber clothing. Cotton burns, but it does not melt into your skin like synthetics.

- Avoid hoodie strings, dangling zippers, or tool lanyards around grinders and drills.

- Wear a leather or canvas shop apron. It contains loose clothing, protects from sparks, and adds a layer of safety.

Every scar has a story. Try not to collect new chapters.

Jewelry

- Remove rings, watches, necklaces, and bracelets before shop work.

- A single ring can cause catastrophic degloving injuries if caught in rotating equipment.

- Even silicone rings, while safer, are best avoided around machinery.

Footwear

- Leather boots are ideal. They resist sparks, hot steel, and sharp dropped pieces.

- Non slip soles matter when quench oil, water, or dust hit the floor.

- Replace worn out footwear. Slick soles are an accident waiting to happen.

Hygiene

- Wash up after handling toxic woods, resins, or oily steels. Dust lingers in beards and hair.

- Keep a dedicated set of shop clothes if you can. Do not bring dust and chemicals into your house or family laundry.

- Consider storing shop only shoes by the door to avoid dragging steel shavings inside.

Practical Shop Notes

- Keep a tray or hook at the shop entrance for rings, watches, and necklaces.

- Dedicate a few sets of clothes to the shop and wash them separately.

- A heavy canvas or leather apron not only protects but also adds a professional feel to your shop routine.

- Keep a spare pair of boots just for the shop. You will avoid tracking metal chips into the house.

- Shower or at least rinse hair and beards after working with exotic woods, fiberglass, or G10.

The best knifemaker is the one who goes home with all his fingers.

Section 7.4 – Working Alone

Knifemaking is often a solitary craft. Many shops are tucked away in garages, basements, or backyard sheds, where it is just you and your tools. Solitude can be one of the joys of the work. There are no distractions, no interruptions, just focus and creation. But working alone also creates risks that many makers do not think about until something goes wrong. Picture this. You are at the grinder late at night, determined to finish a blade. You lose focus for just a moment and the blade catches wrong. Instead of a little nick, the edge slices deep into your hand. Blood is running faster than you expected, and your phone is across the shop on a charger. With someone else there, help would already be on the way. Alone, every second feels longer, and what could have been controlled with quick pressure and a call for help is now a preventable emergency. Or imagine trying to muscle a heavy machine, maybe an anvil or a belt grinder, into a new position. You think you can slide it across the floor on your own. Halfway through, it tips, slips, and suddenly you are pinned awkwardly against the wall. With a buddy, it is a minor mishap. Alone, it is life-threatening, dangerous, and humiliating. The machine does not care how tough you are. It just cares about gravity. And then there is the simplest scenario. You are in the shop for hours and forget to check in with anyone. Your spouse or friends assume you are still tinkering away. But what if you collapsed from heat, fumes, or exhaustion? No one even knows to come looking. A ten second text that says "in the shop, check on me at 9" could be the difference between quick help and hours of silence. These are not just dreadful stories, they are reminders that solo shop time requires extra preparation. Being your own backup plan means thinking ahead. Keep your phone close, set up check ins, make first aid reachable, and know which tasks to avoid when you are alone. With good habits, working alone can still be enjoyable, productive, and safe. The key is respecting that when no one else is there to catch your mistakes, you have to prepare so you do not need them to.

Major Hazards

- Delayed Emergency Response: No one will call 911 or apply first aid if you are incapacitated.

- Falls and Collapses: Slips, fainting from heat, fumes, or exhaustion at the forge.

- Cuts and Burns: Injuries that may seem manageable but become life threatening without help.

- Fires: Sparks or fires can escalate quickly if you cannot respond.

- Isolation: Stress and fatigue are magnified when no one else is present.

Welcome to the shop. Try not to die.

Safe Practices: Preparing to Work Alone

Before You Start

- Check Your Head: If you are tired, stressed, or distracted, do not push it. Working alone with brain fog multiplies every risk.

- Tell Someone: Text or call a spouse, friend, or neighbor. Let them know you are in the shop, and set a time to check back in.

- Emergency Access: Keep doors unlocked or provide a key to someone nearby. Emergency responders lose time breaking in.

- Phone Placement: Have your phone within arms reach, not across the room on a charging cable.

During Shop Work

- Pick Your Tasks Wisely: Avoid the most dangerous solo tasks if you can, such as buffing, heavy forge welding, or ladder work. Save high risk operations for when someone else is around.

- One Hazard at a Time: Do not leave grinders running while you quench steel. Do not walk away from a forge with the blower on.

- Pace Yourself: Fatigue leads to slips. Solo work means taking breaks is non-negotiable.

- First Aid Within Reach: Stock bandages, gauze, and tourniquets where you can reach them quickly.

If Something Goes Wrong

- Call 911 Immediately: Even if you are unsure how bad it is. Operators will guide you step by step.

- Stay Calm, Stay Clear: If it is a fire, your life comes first. Evacuate, then call.

- Self First Aid: Apply pressure, elevate bleeding wounds, and use whatever is closest until you can reach proper supplies.

Extra Layers of Safety

- Check In Timers: Use a simple text system. "In the shop now, check in at 9". If you do not check back, someone comes looking.

- Wearable Tech: Smartwatches or devices with fall detection can auto call help when set up.

- Audible Alerts: Keep a whistle on your bench. It can be easier to blow than yell if injured.

- Signage: Post emergency numbers and your address clearly. If you collapse, rescuers have what they need immediately.

- Fire Preparation: Place extinguishers in easy reach. One at the forge, one by the grinder, one near the exit.

- Use a simple buddy system or safety app that sends an automatic alert if you do not respond to a timer.

Your shop isn't cluttered. It's just a live-action game of "Don't Die."

Practical Shop Notes

- Keep a landline or backup communication option if your shop has bad cell service.

- Store first aid kits in multiple locations. Do not use just one box buried in a cabinet.

- Position tools and benches to avoid climbing, reaching, or awkward maneuvers when solo.

- Leave clear walkways. Tripping hazards are twice as dangerous when no one else is around.

- Keep a spare set of car keys or house keys in the shop in case you need to get out fast.

A clean bench is a happy bench. Yours is currently plotting revenge.

Section 7.5 – Safety Mindset

Every tool in your shop has one thing in common. It does not care who you are. The grinder will not slow down because you have made 500+ knives. The forge does not care how tough you feel. The buffer is not impressed that you have watched hundreds of YouTube tutorials. Tools respond only to respect and caution, and that starts in your head. Confidence is not just helpful in the shop, it is essential. You need confidence to strike steel with authority, to push a bevel against the platen, or to press pins without hesitation. An indecisive mind makes mistakes. Doubt leads to hesitation, and hesitation often leads to inaccuracies. Confidence gives you the steadiness to do good work. But there is a fine line. Confidence grounded in preparation and practice is what makes you a skilled maker. Overconfidence, on the other hand, is what convinces you that safety glasses are optional, that a dust mask is too much trouble, or that you can muscle a grinder into place alone because you have done it before. Arrogance, the attitude that rules do not apply to you, is the quickest way to earn scars. Many seasoned makers will admit their worst injuries did not happen when they were brand new, but after years of doing things the same way. Complacency sneaks in, shortcuts become habits, and respect fades. The shop punishes that kind of mindset quickly. It does not matter how many knives you have made or how many tricks you have learned. The moment you stop respecting the dangers, the dangers will remind you why you should.

That is why a true safety mindset is not about fear, and it is not about pride. It is about balance. Enough confidence to work smoothly, but enough humility to stay cautious. Enough independence to take on challenges, but enough wisdom to ask for help when you need it. A maker who understands balance not only stays safer but also works better, longer, and with more enjoyment.

Major Hazards of a Poor Mindset

- Rushing: Treating shop work like a race. Shortcuts may save minutes but cost months of recovery.

- Overconfidence: Assuming experience makes you immune to mistakes. Even seasoned makers end up in emergency rooms.

- Arrogance: Thinking safety rules do not apply to you because you are better than this.

- Complacency: Letting familiarity dull your awareness. I have done this a hundred times is exactly when mistakes happen.

- Isolation of Knowledge: Refusing to ask for advice or feedback. Pride blocks learning.

- Emotional Work: Entering the shop angry, distracted, or stressed. The wrong mindset for dangerous tools.

- Impairment from alcohol, drugs, or medications: Even legal substances slow reaction time and cloud judgment in a shop full of spinning steel and hot metal.

If your floor is lava, congratulations, you've already lost.

Building a Safety Mindset

Confidence versus Overconfidence

- Confidence is steady. It comes from practice, preparation, and knowing your limits.

- Overconfidence is reckless. It pushes you into tasks without personal protective equipment, skips clamps, or ignores exhaustion.

Rule of Thumb: If you catch yourself saying I will be fine instead of I have prepared, stop and reset.

Slow Down

- Mistakes happen when you rush the small steps, bypassing clamps, ignoring dust masks, or skipping a double check.

- Take pride in the prep work as much as the forging or grinding.

- Thirty seconds of setup is cheaper than three months of physical therapy.

Ask Questions

- Knowledge grows faster when you admit what you do not know.

- Forums, mentors, and even shop buddies are safety nets of experience.

- "I do not know" followed by a question is smarter than "I will figure it out" followed by an injury.

Ask for Help

- Heavy lifts, wiring, or new processes are not solo hero tests.

- Admitting you need another set of hands does not make you weak. It makes you safe.

- Remember an anvil will not praise you for moving it alone, but your back will punish you for weeks.

Humility is Safer

- The shop does not respect arrogance. Prideful shortcuts have sent more makers to hospitals than beginner mistakes.

- Experienced makers get hurt not because they lack skill, but because they forget caution.

- Every project is an opportunity to practice respect for the tools, the materials, and yourself.

Organization is for people who want to keep all ten fingers.

Practical Shop Notes

- Post reminders in your shop. Respect the steel. Respect the tools. Respect yourself.

- Keep a visible checklist for daily routines. Personal protective equipment, ventilation, fire safety.

- Build reflection into your work. After each project, take time to go through what went well and what could have gone wrong.

- Make humility part of your culture. Share your mistakes with other makers so they do not repeat them.

- Balance confidence with caution. Never enter the shop with one and leave the other behind.

That random bolt on the floor has your name on it and a tiny vendetta.

Special Considerations

By now you have covered the core shop safety topics of layout, tools, materials, and personal protection. But shops do not exist in lonely isolation. They are not just places where one person grinds steel alone in perfect silence. They are part of homes, communities, families, and sometimes small businesses. That means safety is not just about you. It is about the people, pets, and responsibilities that overlap with your workspace. This section, Special Considerations, is where we zoom out from sparks and steel to look at the bigger picture. Who else might be in your shop, whether by invitation or accident? How do you prepare for an eager apprentice or a curious neighbor? What happens when your dog wanders in or your kid wants to help? And what about the less visible dangers such as liability, insurance, and the very real possibility of being held accountable if something goes wrong? These special considerations align with OSHA guidelines on visitor safety, home-based workshop liability, and the human-performance side of hazard control. Every experienced maker will tell you the shop is dangerous, but so is complacency. And complacency is not just personal. It is assuming that other people around you will be fine. The hard truth is that most accidents involving visitors or pets are not dramatic explosions or catastrophic fires. They are small moments of oversight such as a trip over a cord, a curious hand reaching for a blade, or a tail knocking something sharp to the floor. This section exists to help you spot those overlooked risks and prepare for them before they become stories that end with regret. Think of Special Considerations as the chapter where you stop being a solo maker and start being a host. Whether you like it or not, when someone enters your shop, even for a five minute look, you are responsible for them. Apprentices bring enthusiasm, but they also bring inexperience. Their mistakes can become your liability. Children and visitors are drawn in by curiosity, but they lack awareness. They do not see danger where you do. Pets offer comfort, but their unpredictability can turn a normal day into an emergency. Insurance and liability may feel like paperwork, but they are the safety net that keeps one accident from costing everything you have built. Ignoring these factors is like leaving your forge unattended to a 6 year old. You might get away with it once, twice, maybe even ten times, but eventually it will catch up with you.

Machines, blades, and chemicals follow predictable rules. People do not. That unpredictability is what makes apprentices, kids, and guests the trickiest part of shop safety. A buffer will not suddenly decide to run across the floor, but a child will. A forge will not sneak up behind you, but a dog might. This section emphasizes setting boundaries early and clearly. It is not because you do not trust people. It is because you know they do not see what you see. Apprentices think they are ready for more than they are. Visitors assume they are just looking. Kids assume if something is glowing it must be magical, not dangerous. Even adults will ask "can I just try it", and your answer has to be consistent, firm, and safe. Safety here is about communication.

> The shop doesn't get mad. It gets even... usually with your kneecap.

It is about turning "no" into an act of care, not rejection. It is about showing others that the most important skill in your shop is not hammering, grinding, or finishing. It is respect. Many makers treat their shops as sanctuaries, but sanctuaries often attract company. Family members pop in, neighbors stop by, pets curl up in corners. These interactions are not bad. In fact they can be a source of connection and joy, but they have to be managed. Children should learn by watching, not touching. With the right guidance they can grow into safe helpers or even future makers, but only if their first lessons are grounded in boundaries. Pets belong in the quiet version of your shop such as hand sanding, sketching, or sweeping. They do not belong when sparks, flames, or dust are flying. Visitors deserve a short briefing. Even a thirty second "freeze if I say so" rule can prevent a serious accident. The lesson here is not exclusion. It is preparation. You can welcome people and pets into your world, but only when you have set the stage for safety first.

There is one more piece makers often avoid thinking about; liability. You may see yourself as a hobbyist, but the law does not. If someone is injured in your shop, even if they ignored every rule you told them, you may be held responsible. If a fire spreads from your garage forge, your homeowner insurance may refuse to cover it because they see it as business use. If a knife you sold fails in use, you could be liable for damages. That does not mean you should live in fear. It means you should live prepared. Liability insurance, small business coverage, and even simple waivers for apprentices or students are tools just as important as a respirator or a fire extinguisher. They do not make you less of a craftsman. They make you a craftsman who takes the long view. Protecting your shop and your livelihood means thinking beyond the workbench.

Special Considerations are about perspective. It reminds us that safety is not just goggles and gloves. It is also foresight and responsibility. It is teaching the apprentice not just how to grind, but why to clamp. It is telling the visitor no, not because you do not trust them, but because you value them. It is recognizing that your dog may love being near you, but that love will not stop a grinder from catching a tail. And it is acknowledging that even the best prepared shop still needs a backup plan if something goes wrong. The work you do matters. The knives, the handles, the craft, it all matters. But the people, pets, and life around your shop matter more. This section exists to help you hold onto both.

"I'll clean it later" is the shop's favorite bedtime story.

Section 8.1 – Apprentices & New Learners

One of the oldest traditions in knifemaking, blacksmithing, and woodworking is apprenticeship. It is the passing down of skills from one set of hands to the next. For centuries this is how crafts survived. Someone with knowledge shared it, often in a dusty shop, with someone eager to learn. That tradition still lives today, whether it is formal apprenticeships or just letting a buddy or family member step in to give it a try. Apprentices bring fresh enthusiasm to the shop. They are curious, energetic, and often fearless. And that is exactly why they are also vulnerable. Enthusiasm does not equal experience. A new learner might not recognize a hazard until they are already in it. To them a grinder looks like a way to make sparks, not a machine that can grab a glove and break bones in an instant. Teaching an apprentice is rewarding, but it changes your role. Your shop is no longer just a workshop. It is a classroom. Every tool, every process, every habit gets passed on, good or bad. If you work with discipline and patience, that is what they will learn. If you cut corners or rush through steps, they will think that is normal too. And here is the catch. Teaching is not just about showing them how to hammer, grind, or quench. It is about teaching them the unglamorous details such as how to clamp properly, when to step back, and why you sweep up dust. These small boring habits are the ones that keep apprentices safe and, in the long run, skilled. An apprentice who learns only the flashy highlights is half trained, and half trained in a knife shop is a dangerous thing. So apprenticeship is not just about skills transfer. It is about responsibility. You are shaping another maker, yes, but you are also shaping their safety culture.

Major Hazards

- Inexperience: New learners often do not understand how fast things can go wrong.

- Split Focus: Teaching requires you to watch their safety as much as your own work.

- Shortcut Temptation: Apprentices may imitate bad habits you do not even realize you have picked up.

- Legal Responsibility: If an apprentice is injured, you may be held accountable, even in a hobby shop.

- Complacency: It is easy to assume they are getting it faster than they actually are.

Safe Practices

Training and Supervision

- Always demonstrate a process fully before letting an apprentice attempt it.

- Stay within arms reach during their early attempts at new tools.

- Do not assume they know better. Even basics need repetition.

- Establish ground rules. No phones, no horseplay, no improvisation without guidance.

Your workbench isn't messy. It's a booby-trapped art installation.

Task Selection

- Begin with shop basics such as sweeping, organizing, labeling tools, and observing.

- Move into hand tools such as files, clamps, and sanding blocks to build understanding.

- Forging under supervision can be introduced early. Apprentices can quickly learn respect for hot steel when striking simple tapers, hooks, or basic shapes. You control the fire, fuel, and quench until they have proven discipline.

- Never allow a beginner at the forge or grinder unsupervised until they show consistent caution and maturity.

- Save the most dangerous jobs such as buffers, advanced grinding, and power hammers for later stages of training.

Teaching With Intention

Apprentices do not just need to know what to do. They need to know how and why. Skipping steps or only showing the fun parts leaves them vulnerable.

- Explain every action. Show how to position clamps, how much pressure to use, and why it matters.

- Narrate your process. As you work, describe your choices.

- Highlight risks in real time. Do not hide mistakes. Use them as lessons.

- Encourage repetition. Mastery comes from repeating small tasks, not rushing into big projects.

- Slow them down. Apprentices want to do the cool stuff immediately. Your job is to show them that patience is a safety (and quality) tool.

- Pass on your mindset. The way you treat safety is the way they will treat safety. If you model discipline, they will mirror it.

PPE and Shop Habits

- Make personal protective equipment mandatory, not optional. From day one, goggles, respirators, and ear protection should be routine.

- Explain hazards behind personal protective equipment. Why the respirator matters, not just that it does.

- Build habits of preparation such as donning personal protective equipment, checking workspaces, and clearing paths.

- Reiterate the mindset of keeping the workshop clean. A cleaner shop is typically a safer shop.

> The grinder doesn't hate you. It just really wants to wear your face.

Liability and Safety Culture

- If the apprentice is under 18, involve parents or guardians in safety discussions.

- Keep notes of what you have taught. Even informal logs show you have emphasized safety. Those logs become invaluable if an injury or litigation is presented.

- Remember you are not just teaching a craft. You are teaching how to work in a dangerous environment responsibly.

Practical Shop Notes

- Keep apprentices away from high risk tools until they show steady judgment.

- Label personal protective equipment so they know what is theirs, and keep it clean.

- Slow your own pace when teaching. Your speed sets the tone.

- Structured beginner projects such as hooks, bottle openers, and sanding blocks let them build skills safely.

- Treat every lesson as if it is being recorded. It makes you deliberate and professional.

Your lathe is basically a spinning middle finger to common sense.

Section 8.2 – Children & Visitors in the Shop

Few things draw more attention than a working shop. For kids the glowing steel of a forge and the spray of sparks from a grinder look like scenes from a storybook. For friends, neighbors, or curious visitors the sight of racks of tools and the smell of hot metal is enough to spark endless questions. A maker's shop can feel like a place of magic. But the truth is it is also a place of risk. Children do not naturally recognize that a dull looking blade can still slice them open or that a piece of steel that looks gray may still be hot enough to burn. Visitors often underestimate just how unforgiving the shop environment is. They think of it as a workshop to browse through, not a place where nearly every surface could cut, crush, or burn them. That does not mean you cannot share your craft. In fact many makers find deep joy in showing others how things are made. It simply means you have to be intentional in how you welcome people into your space. The key is balance. You do not want your shop to feel like a fortress that no one can enter, but you also cannot treat it like your living room. By setting the right tone, firm but friendly, you can invite children and guests into your world without compromising their safety or your focus. This is not about being bossy or unkind. It is about making sure that everyone who comes in also walks out in one piece, with a new appreciation for your craft rather than a trip to urgent care.

The Risks of Curiosity

Children are naturally drawn to glowing steel, moving belts, and sparks. Visitors are the same, especially if they have never been in a working shop before. The danger is that their instincts do not match the hazards around them. A child may lean toward the forge, fascinated by the color, not realizing heat radiates far past the fire. A guest might reach for a blade to admire it, unaware that it is sharper than a razor. And even if they do not touch anything, their presence can divide your attention. Divided attention is one of the fastest paths to accidents.

Setting the Stage: The Two Minute Briefing

Before anyone steps inside your shop, take two minutes to set expectations. This does not have to be harsh or long winded. It just needs to be clear and confident.

"Welcome to the shop. This is an active workspace, so for your safety you will need to wear safety glasses and stay behind the tape line unless I say otherwise. Assume all steel is hot and all blades are sharp. If I say freeze, immediately stop where you are. If anything feels uncomfortable, speak up and we will step back out."

That little speech sets the boundaries, puts you in control, and gives you a tool called freeze to instantly halt motion if needed.

> That cutoff wheel is one bad mood away from turning you into confetti.

Children in the Shop

With kids the safest rule is the younger they are the farther they should stay from the action. Little ones belong at the doorway, not inside. They can watch, they can learn, they can ask questions, but they do not need to be near hot steel or machines. Older children with maturity can step closer under direct supervision but usually still as observers.

A great way to keep kids engaged is to give them a safe job such as timing heats on a stopwatch, counting hammer blows, or sketching what they see. It gives them ownership without risk. And if they get restless escort them out kindly with a positive spin. *"You did great. Now let us watch from the door so we can see everything safely"*.

Visitors in the Shop

Visitors can be trickier than children because they often assume they know enough to try something. Someone will inevitably say *"Can I just try that"*. The safest answer is usually no. That is not you being harsh. It is you keeping them safe. You can explain it plainly like this:

"This tool injures experienced makers. If I cannot give you full attention and training the answer has to be no. I would rather you leave here with all your fingers than with a story."

Most people respect the answer once they hear the reasoning. And you can soften the refusal by giving them safer alternatives, something meaningful but harmless.

Safe Alternatives

When a child or visitor wants to help, redirect them into safe tasks:

- Marking scrap with chalk or soapstone.
- Hand sanding a block of wood.
- Sweeping up non sharp debris in a designated safe zone.
- Turning pages in a sketchbook while you explain a step.
- Taking photos or video from the safe zone with permission.

These alternatives keep people involved without putting them in harm's way.

> The bandsaw is quiet… until it decides to audition for a horror movie.

When to Step Things Back

Sometimes the best choice is to pause the visit or escort someone out. Maybe a child cannot stay still or a guest keeps edging closer than they should. The trick is to do it with care, not confrontation.

"I want to keep showing you this, but it is not safe where you are right now. Let us move back to the door where we can still see everything safely."

This way you maintain authority while keeping the tone respectful.

Key Takeaways

- Visitors and kids are curious, but curiosity does not equal awareness.
- A quick confident briefing keeps you in control and gives clear rules.
- Saying no is a tool. It keeps everyone safe, not insulted.
- Redirecting attention with safe alternatives keeps guests engaged without risk.
- Escorting someone out is not punishment. It is part of responsible hosting.

Belt grinders don't have souls, but they do have excellent aim.

Section 8.3 – Pets in the Shop

Many makers work out of home shops or garages, and that often means pets are not far away. A shop dog may wander in to check on you, or a cat might curl up on a warm windowsill while you are grinding. Some people even think of their pets as unofficial shop mascots. Loyal companions who make long hours at the bench less lonely. They provide comfort, reduce stress, and sometimes make the space feel more alive. But as comforting as they are, pets and shops do not mix easily. The same traits that make them endearing, curiosity, loyalty, and unpredictability, are the very things that can cause trouble. A wagging tail does not recognize sparks from a grinder. A cat sees a workbench as a perch, not a surface full of sharp tools and epoxy. Even the calmest animal can be startled by a loud clang or sudden flare, and in a shop environment one startled leap can create a cascade of danger. It is important to remember that pets experience your shop differently than you do. Their senses are sharper, but not in the ways that help them recognize hazards. They hear noises at volumes we cannot imagine, making hammer strikes and saws feel overwhelming. Their lungs are smaller and more sensitive, meaning a little airborne dust to you might be much more harmful to them. And unlike people, pets do not understand rules. They cannot tell the difference between safe and unsafe zones unless you enforce the boundary for them.

The truth is simple. You can share your space with pets, but you cannot make it pet proof. Enjoy their company during quiet moments such as hand sanding or sketching, but when it comes to forging, grinding, or running machines, pets are better kept out of the shop. Protecting them means protecting yourself, because distraction and unpredictability in a shop are just as dangerous as sparks and steel.

Major Hazards

- Movement Hazards: Pets underfoot can cause trips or slips while you are carrying sharp, hot, or heavy items.

- Heat and Fire: Forges, torches, and hot stock are magnets for burns if a curious nose or paw gets too close.

- Sharp Tools and Chips: Benches, floors, and bins often have razor sharp offcuts that stick to paws or fur.

- Noise and Stress: Grinders, hammers, and saws can frighten pets or even damage their hearing.

- Dust and Chemicals: Fur and small lungs do not handle shop dust or fumes well. Exposure can make them seriously ill.

The drill press is patient. It waits until you're distracted, then collects its toll.

Safe Practices

Boundaries

- Keep pets out of the active work zone when machinery, fire, or chemicals are in use.
- Set up a designated safe space nearby, such as a dog bed outside the shop door or a penned area where they can see you but not interfere.
- Use gates, half doors, or closed doors to prevent surprise entries.

Environment

- Keep the floor clear of cords, scraps, and dropped items. Pets do not know what is sharp until it is too late.
- Store chemicals, resins, and oils on high shelves or in sealed cabinets. Many common shop products are toxic to animals.
- Sweep regularly. Metal shavings, nails, and splinters stick to paws and fur easily.

Awareness and Distraction

- If your pet enters the shop unexpectedly, stop what you are doing immediately. No work is safe when you are distracted by where your dog or cat might wander.
- Avoid multitasking between animal care and active shop work. Feeding, letting them in or out, or giving attention should be separate from operating machinery.
- Remember even well behaved animals can react unpredictably when startled.

First Aid for Pets

- Keep a few basics on hand: saline rinse for eyes, clean cloths for minor cuts, and knowledge of your nearest emergency vet.
- Treat pets like people in one respect. Know your emergency plan before an accident happens.

Practical Shop Notes

- Baby gates or half doors are your best friend for keeping pets close but not underfoot.
- Reserve pet shop time for quiet tasks such as hand sanding, drawing, or cleaning.
- Keep fresh water outside the shop. Heat, dust, and fumes dehydrate animals quickly.
- Treat visitors' pets the same as children. Not near active machinery, and only from a safe observation point.

Your welder is not "a little hot." It's one spark away from a divorce.

Section 8.4 – Liability & Insurance

Knifemaking, blacksmithing, and metalworking are often not just hobbies. Either way they involve risk. You are working with tools and materials that can cause injury, fire, or damage. Most makers spend hours thinking about personal protective equipment, shop layout, and safe practices, but very few think about what happens if something goes wrong beyond a cut or burn. What if a visitor trips and breaks an arm in your shop? What if sparks from your forge ignite part of your garage and spread to your house? What if a knife or tool you gifted or sold fails and injures someone else? These are not fun questions, but they are real ones. And while you can reduce risk with safety practices, you cannot eliminate it. That is where liability and insurance come in.

This section is not meant to shock you. It is meant to prepare you. A little planning can save you from massive financial and legal headaches later. You do not need to be a lawyer to protect yourself. You just need to understand the basics and be proactive.

Major Concerns

- Personal Liability: Injuries to visitors, apprentices, or even delivery people who enter your shop.

- Property Damage: Fires, electrical faults, or water damage caused by shop activities.

- Product Liability: A knife or tool you sell or gift that fails in use and injures someone.

- Business versus Hobby: If you sell your work, even occasionally, your shop activities may legally be treated as a business.

Safe Practices

Protecting Yourself at Home

- Homeowner insurance: Some policies cover fire or property damage from hobbies, but many exclude business activity. Always check your policy and ask your agent directly.

- Riders and add-ons: You may be able to add a small rider to cover shop equipment or liability for visitors.

- Documentation: Keep basic records of your tools, setup, and safety precautions. If something happens, this shows you were not careless.

Liability & Insurance

If You Sell or Teach

- Business insurance: Even if you sell a few knives a year, consider a small business or craft policy. These often cover product liability and injuries at shows or demos.

- Liability waivers: If you teach classes or let others use your equipment, have participants sign a simple waiver. It will not protect you from gross negligence, but it does show they accepted risk.

- Legal structure: For more serious sellers, forming a limited liability company can help protect personal assets if something goes wrong.

Working With Visitors

- Set clear boundaries: As outlined in Sections 8.1 and 8.2, keep visitor areas defined and brief them on safety. Doing so reduces risk and shows due diligence.

- Having them sign a safety sheet or waiver showing the risks were explained can often protect yourself from legal liability claims.

- Maintaining a strong safety mindset is your best defense to legal problems.

First Aid and Emergency Plans

- Document that you have these in place. If something happens, being prepared matters.

Practical Shop Notes

- Review your homeowner or renter policy and ask directly about coverage for shop fires or equipment.

- If you sell knives, even casually, talk to an insurance agent about product liability coverage.

- Keep digital photos of your shop, tools, and layout. These help in claims and also prove you were safety minded.

- A small lockbox or binder with copies of insurance papers, waivers, and emergency contacts should live in the shop or nearby.

- Consider a simple visitor sign-in sheet or digital waiver app for anyone who enters the active shop area. It shows due diligence if anything ever happens.

- There are no sure fire ways to protect yourself from lawsuits and claims. Documentation is the best way to show you have done your due diligence.

- Consistent documentation proves that you are concerned about the safety of others and you are doing everything in your power to keep them safe.

Note: If you do not maintain a steady safety mindset in your shop, you have no protection if anyone else gets injured.

Power tools don't break. They just upgrade to "personal injury mode."

Section 9

Reference Materials

When you are standing in the middle of a busy shop, you do not always have time to think, flip through a book, or search online for safety information. That is where reference materials come in. They are not meant to replace training or experience. They are meant to back you up when memory slips, adrenaline spikes, or fatigue sets in. Every profession has its quick references. Pilots keep laminated cards in the cockpit. Paramedics carry pocket guides. Construction crews post charts in job trailers. Knife making and blacksmithing deserve the same treatment. The tools and materials we handle are unforgiving, and the safest workers are those who know where to look for answers when they need them. This section is built to provide exactly that: wall ready, shop ready, reference material. Every page in this section may be removed, copied, laminated, and displayed wherever it will be most useful in your shop.

Whether it is a checklist by the door, a chart above the grinder, or a quick reference guide next to the first aid kit, these resources keep safety visible. These reference materials align with OSHA guidelines for quick-access safety information in small workshops.

What You Will Find in This Section

- Checklists (9.1): Practical, repeatable steps for daily routines. Pre startup, shutdown, visitor briefings, and first aid supplies.

- Charts (9.2): Hazard information boiled down into tables. Wood toxicity, steel safety, respirator filters, and noise levels. All simplified so you can glance and act.

- Quick Reference Guides (9.3): Concise summaries of common hazards. Fire extinguisher types, first aid basics, chemical symbols, and electrical load rules.

- Emergency Information (9.4): Fill in the blank templates for shop specific details. Emergency contacts, 911 prompts, and evacuation plans.

- SDS Reference (9.5): A plain language introduction to Safety Data Sheets. For many makers, SDS binders feel intimidating, but they are vital.

That pile of oily rags isn't trash. It's a slow-motion fireball with commitment issues.

Why Reference Materials Matter

The truth is simple. Memory fails under stress. In the middle of a fire, you will not remember which extinguisher type to grab. If your eyes are burning from a splash of finish, you will not recall whether to flush for five minutes or twenty. When a visitor wanders into the shop, you might forget to explain the freeze rule until it is too late. Reference materials act as a backup brain. They make the right decision and the easy choice by putting the information right in front of you, when and where you need it. They also act as silent teachers. An apprentice or friend who sees you using a checklist learns that safety is not something you improvise. It is something you build into your routine. A family member who can find the emergency contact sheet knows exactly what to do if they are the one making the call.

Making It Work in Your Shop

- Cut it out. Copy it. Laminate it. Post it. The more visible these references are, the more useful they become.

- Customize it. Fill in your shop emergency contacts, add new charts for unusual woods or chemicals, and update your first aid checklist as your needs change.

- Use it. Do not let these pages collect dust in a binder. Build them into your daily workflow. The goal is not to be overwhelmed with information. It is to make safety information as easy to grab as a hammer or a clamp.

Section 9.1 – Checklists

When you are working in a shop, it is easy to assume you will remember everything. After all, putting on your safety glasses, turning off the forge, or checking the first aid kit seem like obvious steps. But the truth is, when you are focused on your work or when you are tired at the end of a long day, those obvious steps are the first ones to be skipped. That is where checklists come in. Checklists are not about treating makers like beginners. They are about reducing mental load. Pilots use them. Surgeons use them. Electricians use them. Why? Because even experts miss details under pressure, fatigue, or distraction. A simple list on the wall is the difference between thinking you did it and knowing you did it.

This section provides four practical checklists that every shop can benefit from:

- Pre-Startup Shop Checklist

- End-of-Day Shutdown Checklist

- Master Daily Safety Checklist

- Visitor Safety Briefing

- First Aid Kit Supplies

These are not meant to slow you down. In fact they speed you up by building habits. With repetition you will internalize the rhythm, but keeping the lists visible ensures you never get complacent. They also work as a silent teacher: if an apprentice or visitor sees you use them, they learn that safety is routine, not optional. Think of checklists as one of your tools, like your grinder or forge, except this one protects your shop, your work, and your health. And unlike most tools, it costs nothing but a little discipline.

Pre-Startup Shop Checklist

- PPE on: safety glasses, hearing protection, respirator if dust or fumes expected.
- Loose clothing, jewelry, long hair secured.
- Ventilation running (fan, open door, dust collector, etc.).
- Fire extinguisher in place, charged, and visible.
- Electrical cords and outlets checked for damage, no frays or overloading.
- Floor clear of trip hazards (scrap, cords, loose tools).
- Sharp tools stored securely, not left where they can fall.
- Any chemicals or finishes stored with lids tight, not open on the bench.
- First aid kit stocked and reachable.

End-of-Day Shutdown Checklist

- All power tools turned off and unplugged if possible.
- Forge, oven, or torches completely extinguished and cooled.
- Battery chargers and bench lights unplugged (avoid slow-drain fire hazards).
- Flammable rags (oily, solvent-soaked) placed in a sealed metal can.
- The work area was swept, especially dust and metal shavings near outlets or cords.
- Hot steel placed in a safe area if still cooling.
- Fire watch: pause for five minutes to check for smoke, smell of burning, or sparks.
- Lock up or secure dangerous tools if kids or visitors may enter later.
- Take a final walkthrough lap of the shop looking for any potential safety issues.

Wood dust is just the shop's way of giving you a free lung tattoo.

Master Daily Safety Checklist

Use this single sheet every day before you start and after you finish.

Pre-Startup

- PPE on and correct
- Ventilation running
- Fire extinguisher charged and visible
- Floor clear of trip hazards
- Sharp tools stored safely
- First aid kit stockedaaa21

During Work

- One hazard at a time
- No rushing
- Visitors briefed and in safe zone
- Pets out of active area

End-of-Day

- All machines off and unplugged
- Forge/torches cooled
- Flammable rags in sealed can
- Floor swept
- Hot steel marked and in a safe location
- Final visual inspection of entire shop
- Final walkthrough completed

Weekly

- Check SDS binder
- Review visitor logs (if applicable)
- Update first aid kit

Print, laminate, and keep this sheet by the shop door.

Oily rags don't start fires. They throw parties and invite the whole neighborhood.

Visitor Safety Briefing Checklist

- Provide visitor PPE: safety glasses at minimum, hearing protection if noisy.
- Explain that all steel is hot, all blades are sharp.
- Point out a visitor line or zone, where they can stand safely.
- Teach the freeze rule: if you say it, they stop moving immediately.
- Remind them: no touching tools, blades, or materials without permission.
- Show them where to exit if they feel uncomfortable.

Visitor Safety Acknowledgement

I have received the safety briefing above and understand the rules of this shop. I agree to follow them at all times.

- Stay in the designated safe zone.
- Never touch tools, blades, machines, or materials without permission.
- Follow all instructions immediately, including the "Freeze" command.
- Acknowledge that knife making involves real hazards and I am entering the shop voluntarily.

Printed Name: _________________________________ Date: ___________

Signature: _________________________________

Shop Host (you): _________________________________ Date: ___________

Note: This is a sample form only. Keep signed copies on file. For binding legal protection, consult your insurance provider or attorney to customize the wording.

That "harmless" chemical bottle is one loose cap away from a horror story.

First Aid Kit Supply Checklist

(Keep this kit clearly labeled, dust-free, and easy to grab)

- Adhesive bandages in multiple sizes and shapes (not just small strips)
- Sterile gauze pads (various sizes) and roller gauze
- Medical tape (cloth and waterproof) to secure dressings
- Antiseptic wipes or solution for cleaning cuts
- Antibiotic ointment packets
- Burn gel packets or sterile burn dressings
- Elastic wraps for sprains and compression
- Instant cold packs
- Commercial tourniquet (not improvised)
- Eye wash or saline solution
- Disposable nitrile gloves (multiple pairs)
- Trauma shears or heavy-duty bandage scissors
- Tweezers for removing metal slivers and splinters
- Butterfly closures or wound closure strips
- Medical-grade superglue (for minor cuts)
- Finger cots or fingertip bandages
- Triangle bandage (for slings or pressure)
- Emergency contact list and basic first-aid instructions (inside lid)
- Tetanus booster current. Shop injuries often involve dirty metal, rust, or wood

Note: Check expiration dates every six months and restock immediately after use. For a very active shop, consider upgrading to a full ANSI Class B kit.

Dust is patient. It waits years to turn your lungs into a gravel driveway.

Section 9.2 – Charts

The following charts are not exhaustive. They are a practical starting point built around materials and tools commonly found in knife shops. Every shop will vary depending on the types of woods, steels, adhesives, and processes used. As your shop grows, these charts can be expanded to include new products, specialty materials, or unusual consumables. The goal here is quick reference: to provide a wall-friendly guide that reinforces safe practices without digging through books or OSHA databases.

Wood Toxicity Chart – Common Handle Woods

Wood Type	Hazard Level	Potential Hazard	Symptoms / Risks	Precautions
Cocobolo	High	Toxic dust, sensitizer	Rash, asthma, nose/throat irritation	Respirator, gloves, sleeves
Ebony	High	Respiratory irritant	Breathing difficulty, eye irritation	Dust mask, ventilation
Rosewood	High	Sensitizer, oily dust	Dermatitis, wheezing, asthma	Respirator, gloves
Walnut	Medium	Dust irritant	Rash, nasal irritation	Dust mask
Maple	Low	Dust irritant	Minor irritation, cough	Dust mask
Oak	Medium	Tannic acid in dust	Dermatitis, nasal irritation	Respirator recommended

Chisels are great until one decides your thumb looks tastier than the wood.

Wood Toxicity Chart – Exotics & Synthetics

Material	Hazard Level	Potential Hazard	Symptoms / Risks	Precautions
G10 / Micarta	High	Fiberglass/epoxy dust	Severe respiratory irritation, lung damage	P100 respirator, gloves
Carbon Fiber	High	Fiber dust, conductive particles	Skin rash, lung irritation, electrical shorts	P100 respirator, sleeves
Purpleheart	Medium	Toxic dust	Nausea, nose/throat irritation	Dust mask, gloves
Padauk	Medium	Toxic dust	Eye/respiratory irritation, rash	Dust mask
Snakewood	Medium-High	Toxic dust	Allergic reactions	Respirator
Mammoth Ivory / Bone	Medium	Biological dust/odor	Respiratory irritation, infection risk	Dust mask, disinfect work area

Steel Types & Heat-Treat Quick Reference

Steel Type	Hazards in Handling	Notes for Safety
1084 / 1095	Scale and sharp edges after quench	Handle hot steel with tongs, mark cooling steel
O1 Tool Steel	Oil quench = fire hazard	Quench outside or with ventilation
Stainless (AEB-L, 440C)	Chromium fumes during grinding/welding	Respirator with proper filters
Damascus	Multiple alloys = mixed dust hazard	Treat dust as highly toxic; respirator mandatory

Exotic wood is beautiful… and also trying to give you a lifelong allergy.

Respirator Filter Guide

Hazard Type	Recommended Filter Type	Example Label Color
Dust (wood, steel, G10)	P100 / N100 filter	Magenta (P100)
Organic Vapors (epoxy, solvents)	Organic vapor cartridge	Black
Acid Gases (muriatic, flux fumes)	Acid gas cartridge	White
Combination Hazards	Dual filter (P100 + OV/AG)	Multi-color

Noise Level Chart (Tool Hazards)

Tool / Activity	Approx. dB	Risk Level	Required PPE
Normal conversation	60–65 dB	Safe	None
Drill press	85–90 dB	Hearing risk after 2 hrs	Ear plugs
Belt grinder	95–100 dB	Risk within 30 min	Ear muffs/plugs
Power hammer	105–110 dB	Risk within 5 min	Ear muffs
Forge blower / fans	80–85 dB	Low but cumulative risk	Plugs if prolonged
Angle grinder	110+ dB	Immediate risk	Heavy-duty ear protection

Epoxy glues fingers faster than it glues handles. Ask me how I know.

Section 9.3 – Quick Reference Guides

This subsection provides fast, one-page safety references designed to hang on shop walls, sit in binders, or be laminated for daily use. These are not long explanations. They are distilled, practical guides that let you act quickly and safely when something happens. The goal is to make safety information as visible and accessible as the tools on your bench. Each guide is organized to cover common hazards and responses in a clear, easy-to-read format.

Fire Extinguisher Types & Uses

Type	Label Color	Best For	Do NOT Use On
Class A	Green	Wood, paper, cloth	Flammable liquids, electrical
Class B	Red	Flammable liquids (oils, solvents)	Electrical fires
Class C	Blue	Electrical fires	Safe for energized equipment
Class D	Yellow	Combustible metals (magnesium, titanium)	General fires
Class K	Black	Cooking oils/grease	Metals, solvents

Rule of thumb: In most shops, an ABC-rated extinguisher covers nearly everything. Keep more than one within easy reach.

The bandsaw doesn't cut wood. It cuts corners... and occasionally fingers.

First Aid Basics – Quick Response

Injury	First Steps	When to Seek Help
Cuts / Bleeding	Apply pressure with clean gauze; elevate limb	If bleeding does not stop in 10 min, call 911
Burns (minor)	Cool with running water 10–20 min, cover with clean dressing	If blistering, deep tissue, or large area burned
Burns (major)	Call 911 immediately, cover loosely with clean cloth, do NOT apply ointments	Always
Eye injury (dust/particle)	Flush with eye wash for 15 min	If irritation persists
Eye injury (chemical)	Flush with eye wash 20+ min, remove contacts	Call 911 if severe
Heat exhaustion	Move to cool area, hydrate	If vomiting, confusion, or fainting occurs
Heat stroke	Call 911 immediately, cool body with wet cloths	Always

Woodturning is 10% skill and 90% "please don't take my hand."

Chemical Storage Symbols & Meanings

Symbol	Meaning	Precautions
	Biohazard	Gloves, sealed containers
	Toxic	Respirator, proper ventilation
	Flammable	Store away from sparks, sealed containers
	Oxidizer	Keep away from flammables
	Corrosive	Use acid-resistant containers, gloves
	Gas under pressure	Secure cylinders, store upright

Always read Safety Data Sheets (SDS) for chemicals used in your shop.

This is not an exhaustive list of symbols and hazards. Review SDS Sheets for reference.

Research any unknown symbols for full understanding.

Glue fumes don't make you high. They just make you optimistic about bad decisions.

Electrical Load Quick Guide

Cord Gauge	Max Amps	Typical Use
16 AWG	10 A	Light duty (lamps, fans)
14 AWG	15 A	Medium duty (small tools, short cords)
12 AWG	20 A	Heavy duty (grinders, saws, forges)
10 AWG	30 A	Extra heavy duty (welders, compressors)

Never daisy-chain power strips or run grinders on Christmas light cords.

Lockout / Tagout (LOTO) Quick Reference

Lockout/Tagout is required any time you service, clean, or repair equipment that has stored energy (electrical, mechanical, hydraulic, pneumatic, etc.).

- Step 1: Notify anyone who could be affected.
- Step 2: Shut off the machine and isolate the energy source.
- Step 3: Apply your personal lock and tag to the energy-isolating device.
- Step 4: Verify the machine is de-energized (try to start it).
- Step 5: Perform the work.
- Step 6: Remove lock and tag, restore energy, notify everyone.

Never remove someone else's lock. Never bypass LOTO "just this once."

Finishing oils are like that friend who seems chill until they set you on fire.

Section 9.4 – Emergency Information

Emergencies do not wait for you to dig through your phone, look up numbers, or try to remember your plan. When something goes wrong, seconds matter. This section provides ready-to-fill templates that you can customize for your own shop. Post them somewhere visible near the shop door, first aid kit, or fire extinguisher so you or anyone else in the shop knows exactly what to do and who to call. These pages are not long essays. They are fill-in-the-blank safety tools.

Emergency Contacts Template

Post in a visible spot near your shop entrance.

Contact	Number
Fire Department	
Police Department	
Ambulance / EMS	
Poison Control	
Local ER / Hospital	
Family Contact #1	
Family Contact #2	
Vet (if pets are in the shop)	

Tip: Write them out. Do not just rely on your cell phone. Phones fail. Paper does not.

Notes: (including any vital information. Example: medications, allergies, etc…)

____

____

____

____

Band-aids are not a personality. They're a cry for help with adhesive.

911 Quick Reference

What to tell the dispatcher if you call 911:

1. Location: Exact shop address.

Shop Address:____

2. Nature of emergency: Fire, injury, chemical spill, etc.

3. Condition of injured person(s): Breathing, conscious, bleeding.

4. Hazards present: Fuel, forge, gas tanks, etc.

5. Call-back number: Shop phone or cell.

Phone Number:____

Use your own phone number if you are calling for an injury to someone else.

The operator will guide you step by step. The operators are trained to guide you through the emergency. There is no need to be anxious, use the help available.

Do not hesitate to call, even if you are unsure.

Reminder: It is better to call 911 and not need it than to hesitate and wish you had called.

Example Emergency Plan

Evacuation Routes	Main exit:
	Secondary exit:
Assembly Point	Where everyone meets outside:
Fire Response	• Use an extinguisher if it is safe.
	• Evacuate immediately if fire grows.
Medical Response	• Apply first aid.
	• Call 911 if needed.
	• Stay with the injured person until help arrives.
Special Notes	• Flammable storage location:
	• Compressed gas cylinders location:
	• Electrical shutoff switch location:

:

That "tiny cut" is just warming up for its Oscar-winning infection scene.

Section 9.5 – Quick Reference: Safety Data Sheets (SDS)

A Safety Data Sheet (SDS) is the manufacturer's official safety guide for a chemical, adhesive, resin, or other potentially hazardous material. It is not optional paperwork. It is your cheat sheet for staying safe. Every product sold in the U.S. that has chemical hazards must, by law, come with an SDS. Suppliers are required to provide it on request, and most post them online for free download. This page is not meant to teach you how to become a chemist. It is meant to show you how to actually use SDS sheets in the shop.

Where to Find SDS Sheets

Source	How to Get It
Manufacturer website	Search the product name + SDS
Supplier catalogs	Knife supply shops, resin sellers, steel suppliers often host SDS links
General databases	OSHA and other safety bodies host large SDS libraries
Ask directly	By law, a supplier must provide an SDS within a reasonable time if you request it

How to Read an SDS

Section	What It Tells You
Section 2 – Hazards	Identifies if the material is flammable, toxic, corrosive, etc.
Section 4 – First Aid Measures	What to do if it gets on your skin, in your eyes, or inhaled
Section 7 – Handling & Storage	Storage temperatures, container types, and incompatibilities
Section 8 – Exposure Controls / PPE	Recommends PPE: respirators, gloves, goggles
Section 10 – Stability & Reactivity	Conditions that make it unstable (heat, sparks, mixing with other chemicals)
Section 13 – Disposal Considerations	How to legally and safely get rid of leftovers

Eye wash is for people who thought "I'll be fine" was a safety plan.

Why Keep SDS in the Shop and proper usage

- Emergencies: If someone is injured, paramedics will ask what chemical was involved. Having the SDS handy speeds treatment.

- Liability: Shows you took safety seriously if anything ever goes wrong.

- Memory aid: You do not have to remember storage temps or disposal instructions.

- Keep a binder or digital folder labeled SDS - Shop with every chemical you use.

- Print a cover sheet with a list of products and page numbers for fast lookup.

- Add new SDS sheets as soon as you bring in any new chemical.

- Laminate the SDS cover sheet and keep it on the front of the binder for instant reference

www.ingramcontent.com/pod-product-compliance
Lightning Source LLC
Chambersburg PA
CBHW080937120726
48003CB00011B/3187